The **Autobiography** of
Joseph A. Bagnall

ADVENTURES IN EDUCATION

The **Autobiography** of
Joseph A. Bagnall

ADVENTURES IN EDUCATION

Joseph A. Bagnall

iUniverse, Inc.
New York   Bloomington

The **Autobiography** of
Joseph A. Bagnall

ADVENTURES IN EDUCATION

iUniverse books may be ordered through booksellers or by contacting:

iUniverse
1663 Liberty Drive
Bloomington, IN 47403
www.iuniverse.com
1-800-Authors (1-800-288-4677)

ISBN: 978-1-4401-3432-6 (pbk)
ISBN: 978-1-4401-3433-3 (ebk)

Printed in the United States of America

iUniverse rev. date: 5/18/2012

Cover photo by Melinda Finn, 2011

Dedication
To My Family, Past, Present, and Future

Contents

Foreword

There may not be a tombstone or a final resting place; my ashes will probably be scattered in a favorite place. But my extended epitaph will live in my autobiography.

This book has some pictures and documents that are faded and perhaps offensive to the generation that is blessed with the sharp definition of the digital age. They are included because in their perfunctory way, they help in telling my story.

I have chosen to refer to Fullerton Junior College as Fullerton College, the name it has used for many years since-1970, the last year I served on the faculty. I have a personal aversion to the title junior college, because in reality the transfer courses offered at community colleges are in no way inferior to those offered at four year colleges and universities. As a matter of fact we have statistics to prove that our transfers do better in their junior years than students who enter the university system as freshmen.

As faculty representative from FJC, to the Faculty Association of California Community Colleges (FACCC), I introduced a resolution asking that "junior" be dropped from the titles of all community colleges that were still using it. The resolution passed overwhelmingly.

Joseph A. Bagnall
Oceanside, California
March 2009

Acknowledgments

I am deeply grateful for the support and assistance of my wife, Naomi, and my daughter, Ashley.

Cherish Denton and Steve Furr were the central figures in the production of my book. Many thanks to them for their splendid work!

Progenitors

Florence Noland Bagnall

Florence Noland Bagnall
February 11, 1907—January 1, 1992

These are the facts concerning my best known progenitors. I am **indebted** to my fine mother, Florence Noland Bagnall, for preserving most of the material about my ancestors in her published *Bagnall Family History.* Mother was also the editor for the Sanpete County, Utah, centennial history titled *These Our Fathers.* In addition she wrote a historical novel titled *Let My People Go,* a tale that takes place in Yugoslavia during World War II.

As a young girl, Florence Noland was an organist in a silent movie theatre in Provo, Utah. As an adult, she played for countless church and Mormon temple services, funerals, weddings, and memorial services for World War II heroes---all without a fee.

Mother was a gracious hostess, opening up her home to good friends, her children's friends, and officials of her church and her political party.

As wife of a Utah State legislator she entertained the Governor and his wife in our home As editor of the centennial history of Sanpete County, she received recognition and praise from the President of the Church of Jesus Christ of Latter-day Saints.

I reflect on my mother's radiant beauty, and I am grateful to her for providing a good home and serving as a model for my own life. (Appendix I).

Joseph Bagnall

Born December 27, 1839 in Wakefield, Yorkshire, England, my Great Grandfather, Joseph Bagnall was the son of George Bagnall, an illiterate worker in an English iron foundry, and Ann Rawling.

Joseph married Sarah Ann Frobisher, daughter of Thomas Frobisher and Ann Cookson, on his birthday, December 27, 1864. The newlyweds were English Mormon converts who, at ages 25 and 24, respectively, sailed the Atlantic to America and traversed the plains in a covered wagon ox train. They arrived in present day Salt Lake City, Utah, with the Mormon Henson Walker Company on November 9, 1865.

Joseph and Sarah Frobisher Bagnall
were Mormon pioneers who arrived in Utah in 1865.

Joseph and Sarah settled in Moroni, Utah, in December, 1865. Joseph worked as a stone cutter on the Mormon temple in St. George, Utah. In 1876 the couple relocated five miles away in Chester, Utah. In this new community, Joseph served as a school trustee for 15 years, as a first counselor to Bishop Christensen for 14 years, as owner of a community store, and as a stone cutter for the building of the Manti Temple and the Chester community church. He also built his own stone house in 1889.

The Bagnall House was built in 1889 in Chester, Utah. L to R Horses May and Ben, workman Andy Rassmussen, William H. Bagnall, son of Joseph and Sarah Bagnall, Sarah and Joseph, dog Bruin, and horse Maud, hitched to a buggy.

Water for this home was obtained from an old fashioned well that was plumbed into a kitchen pump. The pump had to be primed with water in order to create a vacuum and initiate the flow.

The house had a parlor with a fireplace, a family organ, a dresser with a marble top, and a large mirror. The cellar beneath the house was stocked with potatoes and other food supplies.

As a small boy in about 1938, I remember exploring the remnants of the old stone house. I recall seeing bright colors (burgundy) in what must have been the parlor.

Although I never had the privilege of knowing my great grandfather, I am told by my father, Joseph R. Bagnall, that he loved music, played the violin and the organ, which he kept in his home, and on occasion he served as a chorister in his church. My father also told me that he owned and operated a small country store. He was a Democrat who was preoccupied with political issues. He was also a Mormon pioneer who prayed with passion, faith, and conviction. Every prayer, I am told, included a plea for "a contented mind."

My paternal grandmother, Hannah Christensen Bagnall, told me that great-grandfather had a subscription to Joseph Pulitzer's *New York World* and to a British newspaper. According to her account, he was sensitive and intelligent. My father believed that if he had lived in a later period in America, he might have become a college professor. In the world of his day he was destined to make fundamental contributions to his family and his posterity as a stonecutter and a counselor to a Mormon Bishop.

Joseph Frobisher Bagnall

Joseph Frobisher Bagnall was the third child born to Joseph and Sarah Ann Frobisher Bagnall. He attended school in a log school house in Chester, Utah, where split logs were used as benches. Students wrote on slates and wood shingles. The latter were erased with a pocket knife. Joseph finished fourth grade.

Joseph F. teamed with his brother William Henry to develop a farm and cattle and sheep ranch. The large livestock enterprise commenced when Joseph F. agreed to be a herdsman for a few years and to take his pay from the owner in sheep. Joseph loved to work with cattle and sheep, while William preferred to till the land and irrigate. Together they built a business known as "Bagnall Brothers." Joseph F. and William were the only children of Joseph and Sarah Ann Bagnall to survive to maturity.

When Joseph F. was 26 years old, he married Hannah Christensen, aged 16 years. Their wedding day was December 1, 1896. On October 23, 1900, Joseph Rodley, their only surviving child, was born. Years later they adopted and raised a child named Jean.

In 1909 Joseph F. accepted a call to go on a Mormon mission to England. His wife Hannah and son Joseph Rodley were left to attend to the duties on the ranch for the next two years. William Henry assumed enormous responsibilities for the operation of Bagnall Brothers in that period.

As a missionary, Joseph F. was Branch President of the Rochdale Branch and later President of the Hyde Branch of the Church of Jesus Christ of Latter-day Saints in England. His missionary journal is filled with repetitive information about study sessions, tracting, holding church meetings, making converts, and visiting friends of the faith.

In 1918 Uncle Will passed away at age 46. He was a

Hannah Christensen Bagnall and Joseph F. Bagnall on their wedding day, December 1, 1896.

victim of the worldwide influenza epidemic. My grandfather was then required not only to manage the entire Bagnall Brothers enterprise, but also to care for William Henry's widow and five children.

Joseph Frobisher Bagnall

During the years 1923-25, grandfather served as a Sanpete County representative in the Utah State Legislature. He was a conservative Republican in the Harding-Coolidge years.

In1924 he was ordained a Mormon Bishop; he presided over the Chester ward for ten years. In this period he also served as a director of the Bank of Moroni. By 1926 he had acquired a herd of 3000 sheep and 200 head of Herford cattle, along with grazing land in Scofield, Milford, and Chester, Utah. This enterprise prospered from 1926 through 1929

From 1929 through 1940, the Bagnall enterprise suffered through the Great Depression, but my grandfather, his nephew, Rawlin Bagnall, and his son, Joseph Rodley, held it together.

Joseph F. Bagnall died on May 10, 1942, on a 1400 acre ranch in Chester, Utah, the place he loved above any other.

Joseph F. Bagnall on the Chester ranch

Joseph Rodley Bagnall

Born three years before the Wright brothers made their famous flight, Joseph Rodley Bagnall's life covered a period when automobiles replaced horse drawn buggies, air travel evolved into space travel, and rural America became, for the most part, urban America.

Joseph Rodley attended a country elementary school in Chester, Utah. His high school days were spent at Snow Academy in Ephraim, Utah.

Florence Noland and JRB in 1928

My father married Florence Noland of Mt. Pleasant, Utah, in 1927. Soon thereafter he finished his Bachelor's Degree at University of Utah and began teaching at an elementary school in Salem, Utah.

During the early part of the Great Depression he taught at Hamilton Elementary School in Mt. Pleasant and at Moroni High School. While teaching history and social science at Moroni High, he studied part time at the University of Utah in order to prepare for a career in educational administration. In 1939 he was hired as Superintendent of the North Sanpete School District, a position he held until he resigned in 1945, In order to help his cousin Rawlin Bagnall, operate the family ranch in Chester.

JR Bagnall Superintendent
Enn Ess Aitch
The North Sanpete High School annual for 1940.

From 1945 to 1948, my father served as Bishop of the Mt. Pleasant North Ward, and later as President of the North Sanpete Stake (comparable to a Catholic diocese).

In 1951 he was serving as a Sanpete County Representative in the Utah State legislature, when church officials appointed him Manager of the Southern California Latter-day Saint Welfare Ranch in Perris, California. Originally this ranch had been developed as an elegant retreat for Louis B. Mayer of Metro Goldwin Mayer movie fame. It had a race track and splendid accommodations for Mr. Mayer's guests and his horses. The property was then sold to the Statler Hotel interests and later purchased by the Mormon Church.

As Manager, Joseph R. directed and supervised planting of alfalfa and row crops and raising of cattle, chicken and hogs. Each Saturday from fifty to one hundred people would arrive from one of the stakes of Southern California. They would come to the ranch and spend the day working on their special stake welfare project. Most stake projects involved the planting, maintaining and harvesting of agricultural produce. During the week the ranch was sustained by five or six permanent families in residence.

In 1953 my father began his study for a Master's Degree, which he obtained from Claremont College in 1955. From 1955 to 1956, he served as Director of Adult Education in the Arcadia Unified School District. From 1956 to 1966 he served as the first Principal of the newly built Richard Henry Dana Middle School in Arcadia, California.

From 1966 to 2001, he lived in retirement in Provo, Utah, where he and mother opened their fine home to six grandchildren who, in turn, each lived there, receiving free room and board, and much loving care, while attending Brigham Young University.

At age 100 my father had a gala party with numerous family members and friends. His centenary year was also marked with a 1/4 page spread in the Provo, Utah *Daily Herald* (Appendix II).

Joseph R. Bagnall 100th birthday

Joseph R. Bagnall died May 27, 2001, at the age of 100 and seven months. He was a good father and grandfather, an educator, and an effective public leader.

Joseph Albert Bagnall

Chapter One: Birth and Early Life

I was born in the Hughes Hospital at Spanish Fork, Utah, on January 15, 1930. My parents were Joseph Rodley (Appendix II) and Florence Noland Bagnall. (Appendix I) Our family lived in Salem, Utah, a small hamlet where my father was employed as an elementary school teacher.

In 1932 I contracted polio, which left my right leg paralyzed for a period of six months. The condition was diagnosed by two competent physicians. My parents said that the leg was healed as a result of the faith exercised in a prayer circle, in the Manti Temple of the Church of Jesus Christ of Latter-day Saints. This much seems certain-- I did experience a bout with polio at age two. I somehow recovered the use of my right leg, and I have lived the balance of my life with no residuals.

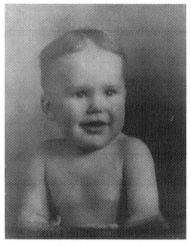

Joseph A Bagnall age 2

I was also in my second year, when on New Year's Day, our family was blessed with the birth of my sister, Marilyn Rae. Marilyn had many friends in her youth. She married Neil P. Richards in 1953, and became an outstanding mother who raised a fine family. Her eldest son Neil served a two year Mormon mission, earned his Ph.D. and became a college professor. Dana served as a missionary, earned his college degree and served as a policeman, and later as a fireman. Lisa attended BYU, raised a fine family and became a very successful real estate agent. Stephen served a two year Mormon mission, earned

Joseph A. in his Indian head dress made by his father.

his law degree and became an attorney. Jon earned his BA and became a very successful CEO. Bryan served a two year Mormon mission, earned a degree as a mechanical engineer, worked successfully in his field, and is a published writer.

Marilyn was not only the central figure in the raising of her children, but she also gave countless hours of assistance to her parents when they were elderly and infirm.

Marilyn Rae and Joseph Albert

211

Marilyn Rae and Joseph A. in 1940

Soon after Marilyn's birth our family moved to Mt. Pleasant, Utah, where my father was employed as a teacher at Hamilton Elementary School. In the summer time we returned to our home in Chester, Utah, where my father helped his father, Joseph Frobisher Bagnall, and his cousin, Rawlin Bagnall, oversee the cattle drive to the mountain range, the lambing season, and the work of the nine man summer hay crew.

In 1935 our family spent one summer in Salt Lake City. We accompanied my father as he began his studies at the University of Utah in educational administration. I had a wonderful experience with the "city kids" in a preschool class. But when my father returned to the University each successive summer through 1938, I found myself living with my grandparents, with my first full time job on the family ranch in Chester. Beginning at age six I spent my summers riding the hay horse eight hours a day, six days a week, as part of a nine man hay crew. The work hours were from 8 am to 5 pm with one hour for lunch. I was paid $.50 a day.

The overall task for the summer hay crew was to stack hay in numerous pasture feed yards and in two barns. Three large hay wagons, each drawn by a team of two heavy draft horses, would furnish a steady supply of hay. Men in the fields would pitch hay into the wagons.

If we were stacking the hay in a feed yard, a wagon would pull up to the spot where the stack would be made. Hovering over the spot would be a derrick, rigged together with pine poles. The derrick was constructed, in form and function, to resemble an industrial crane. On the tip of the derrick was a pulley that accommodated a cable that was fastened to a four foot wide Jackson fork with huge, thick tines. The cable extended from the Jackson Fork back to the lower end of the derrick pole, downward to the derrick base, and outward where it was attached to the harness of a heavy draft horse named Jack. I was perched in an uncomfortable cavalry saddle on "Old Jack", and on command of the teamster on the hay wagon I would turn the horse and ride back toward the hay wagon, lowering the Jackson Fork down to the teamster. He in turn would tromp the huge fork down into the hay, lock it in place, and shout "take it away." I would then ride the horse in the opposite direction, pulling a large portion of the hay load into the air where the stacker would stick a pitch fork into it and guide the hay into the spot where he wanted it dumped. When he found that spot, he would shout "dump it" and the teamster would pull a trip rope fastened to the Jackson Fork and the hay would fall into place. When I heard the command "dump it" I turned the horse around and rode back toward the hay wagon. At this juncture it was dramatic to see the derrick pole sway back through the air and the Jackson Fork descend toward the teamster and his load of hay. I felt a sense of power as the cable fastened to my horse whirred noisily through the pulleys on the derrick. I was proud to know that I was an essential part of the hay crew. But after repeating this process again and again, day after day, week after week, throughout the summer months, I was secretly hoping for anything that might disrupt this monotonous routine. Summer rain was my friend, because due to spoilage problems, we could not stack wet hay.

Pulling the hay into our two barns was even more challenging. I was placed in an *isolated spot* in the back of the barn where I rode back and forth, beating out a dusty trail day after day. I could hear the commands of the teamster and the stacker, but for most of the long day there was not a human face in sight. When one hay rack pulled away, another with a full load pulled into its place in the front of the barn. I therefore rarely got off my horse until lunch time (called dinner time in Sanpete—the evening meal was called supper time) or at "quitting time" at 5 pm.

The summer months brought a long stretch of daylight between quitting time and sundown. Sometimes I didn't have to go to the pasture to round up the "milk cows" and help with the milking. When it was possible, it was great fun to visit my cousins, Grace and Carol Peterson. Sometimes we would go hunting asparagus that grew wild along the ditch banks. Once we went fishing for minnows in a meadow stream, and one time we had a cookout with mutual friends in the evening. We made a bonfire under the trees, roasted potatoes in the fire, enjoyed some good food, hearty laughter and an abundance of genuine fun.

It was always fun when my grandparents took me to the "Kozy Theatre" in nearby Moroni to see some good movies. I enjoyed Tarzan pictures, or Dick Tracy serials that ran as short subjects, or "Our Gang" comedies. I especially enjoyed two movies about Thomas Edison, "Young Thomas Edison," starring Mickey Rooney, and a movie about Edison's adult life, staring Spencer Tracy.

By the time I was 11 years old I was promoted to being a teamster in the field and I began to tromp hay in the hay wagons as well. Shortly after this, during late spring, before the haying season, I became a herdsman and assumed many adult responsibilities in trailing cattle and herding sheep. I spent my childhood summers, therefore, living with grandparents on the Chester Ranch, engaged in grim ranch tasks.

Six day work weeks and church meetings every Sunday were overwhelming to me and I looked forward to summer's end and the opening of school, especially in the academic year of 1939 and 1940. My father's summer studies at the University of Utah had resulted in his appointment as Superintendent of the North Sanpete School District, and as a nine year old boy I had a new home in Mt. Pleasant, Utah, where I entered fourth grade at Hamilton Elementary School.

The Bagnall home in Mt. Pleasant, Utah

Grades one through three at Lincoln Elementary School in Moroni, Utah, had been uneventful, but I did receive a good foundation in basic education there. In third grade I loved my teacher, Cleopha Christensen, and I was captivated by Mark Twain's *Tom Sawyer* and a book called *Thunder Cave*. My heroes were the players on the Moroni High School basketball team. I suppose that it wasn't just a phase of my impressionable childhood, because in my eightieth year I still have a vivid recollection of Bruce Irons, Gideon Jolley, Boyd Anderson, Reece Jamison and Garnell Blackham playing basketball in their handsome blue uniforms with white numerals bordered in red, and the name *Buccaneers* emblazoned on their warm-up jackets in fancy script.

While living in Moroni I took private lessons on the clarinet. As a third grader I played clarinet in the Lincoln Elementary School marching band. In fourth grade, I also played clarinet in the marching band, but this time it was at Hamilton, my new elementary school---and the basketball players at North Sanpete High School became my new heroes. Elmer Fillis and Neldon Jensen were prominent among them.

I spent the last years of my childhood and most of my adolescence, age nine through seventeen, in Mt. Pleasant, Utah. My new home was sometimes referred to as "Hub City" because it was located in the center of the State of Utah. It was also nestled between the Skyline Drive and the majestic Horse Shoe Mountain on the east, and the village of Wales and Box Canyon on the West. Surrounded by towns with poetic names such as Spring City, Fountain Green, Fairview, Moroni, and Indianola, it shared the distinction, along with Ephraim and Manti, of being one of the three largest towns in Sanpete County.

Founded by Mormon pioneers in 1852, Mt. Pleasant was incorporated in 1868, grew to 3000 residents in 1900, and dwindled slightly in the census of 2000. It was religiously and culturally the most diverse settlement in Sanpete County, owing to the fact that Mormon thought was challenged in 1875 with the building of Liberal Hall and the establishment of Presbyterian sponsored Wasatch Academy, Utah's oldest boarding school.

In the 1940s there was not much excitement in the town. Radio, movies, newsreels, and the daily newspapers kept us in touch with the outside world. The big event occurred every day at 4:00 p.m. when the Rio Grande Western passenger train arrived from southern Utah, en route to Salt Lake City. Freight trains used the same route, and as early as 1930 townsmen had enjoyed the advantage of travel on an intercity bus. Ironically at the turn of the 21st Century, there was neither rail nor bus service connecting Mt. Pleasant to other places in the state.

Our Mt. Pleasant home had a studio apartment in the back yard, which we attempted to rent for $5 per month, but even when we offered to pay the utilities, it was difficult to find people who could afford these terms. Economic conditions were still bleak in 1939, during the last desperate years of the Great Depression.

On September 1, 1939, I remember seeing the banner headline on our morning *Salt Lake Tribune* about Germany invading Poland. Our teacher in fourth grade told us that this could be the beginning of a second world war in Europe. I also remember the baritone twang of Elmer Davis as he reported the events of the war on network radio. Soon thereafter Edward R. Murrow began his short wave transmissions from London, carried on KSL and the CBS Radio Network. Murrow would always begin his dramatic newscasts with, "This is London...." The signal was always plagued with static from his short wave rig, and in the background you could hear the bombs of the German Luftwaffe, anti-aircraft guns firing, air raid sirens blaring, and other sounds of war. He described the Battle of Britain and the heroic stand of Winston Churchill and the English people in a time when the fascist powers--Germany, Italy and Spain-- controlled continental Europe and Britain stood alone.

But the war in Europe was far away and life in Mt. Pleasant was simple, serene, and secure. It was time for new adventures in our new surroundings. Behind our studio apartment stood a red carriage barn that dated back to the early part of the 20th Century, or perhaps the late part of the 19th. The barn had wooden floors with an upper and lower level. There was enough space to park two cars on the lower level, while the slightly elevated upper level could be used for basketball games. My father and I put up a backboard and a basket and created a mini gymnasium for small kids. Many happy hours were spent with elementary school friends there. If the weather was hot, we opened a large sliding door that extended across the width of our gym. In the frigid winter months we slid the door shut and practiced in our covered facility with little regard for severe weather conditions outside.

On Sunday, December 7, 1941, I was playing basketball in the carriage barn with a few sixth grade friends, when a neighbor rushed in, stopped the game, and announced that Japan had attacked the Pacific fleet in Pearl Harbor and our country was now at war. We were shocked! But we would have been terrified if we had known the full extent of our naval losses in the Pacific. The next day President Roosevelt asked the Congress for a declaration of war against Japan. His strong, confident voice rang out with words that both his supporters and detractors believed. "We will win the inevitable victory" he said, "so help us God."

The academic year of 1941-42 was my last at Hamilton Elementary School. I remember the posters in our sixth grade classroom, urging everyone to buy war bonds. Even elementary students bought war stamps that they pasted in booklets that would eventually add up to $18.75. At maturity this amount became a $25 war bond. Ration books were issued to our families for various food items, and stickers displayed on automobile windshields indicated the allotment of gasoline the family could consume each week. Casualty lists appeared in newspapers along with reports that local men had been captured and were in Japanese prison camps. I saw, firsthand, young men who had been deprived of material comforts in the Great Depression, enlisting or being drafted to fight in World War II. I saw my friends lose members of their families, and I remember my father, Superintendent of Schools, wearing the uniform of the Home Guard, around town and on trips to the city.

Tom Brokaw, former anchor for NBC Nightly News, has written an important book titled *The Greatest Generation*. He was correct when he ranked the generation that defeated the Great Depression and won World War II as the finest America has produced. As I say this, I must simultaneously issue a disclaimer. I was too young to make any significant contribution to the defeat of the depression or the winning of World War II, but I witnessed the courage and commitment of the American people who served in uniform, worked in war industries and sacrificed on the home front. They coped magnificently with the successive crises of economic collapse and a massive worldwide war. We were fortunate, I have since discovered, to have the bold leadership of one of America's greatest presidents—Franklin D. Roosevelt.

Chapter Two: Adolescence

The academic year 1942-1943 began in the North Sanpete High School building where the junior high grades (7th, 8th, and 9th) were housed with the senior high school. It was a special thrill to attend senior high school assemblies, pep rallies, "at home" athletic contests, and to study in proximity to my high school role models. My dual citizenship also included the privilege of playing in the high school band.

North Sanpete Junior and Senior High School in Mt. Pleasant, Utah

I remember collecting the popular 78 rpm "boogie" and swing records of the day. Much of my record collection was acquired from the town's teen age hangout, a malt shop named 4C after the proprietor Mr. Forsey. When the records on the 4C juke box fell off the weekly hit parade list, I was able to pick up these discards for a nominal price. Many of them still spin in my head. How can one ever forget Glen Miller, Harry James, Tommy Dorsey, Benny Goodman, The Mills Brothers, Johnny Mercer, Perry Como, Bing Crosby, Judy Garland, Betty Hutton, the Andrews Sisters, and the incomparable Frank Sinatra?

I inherited an old wind--up phonograph that could be closed up and carried like a suitcase. I modified it by installing an electric turntable and pickup, and hooking it through an old table-model Philco radio.

My home-made contraption was great for listening to records in my room. It was also portable, and I took it to church-sponsored youth meetings where it furnished music for our dances and parties.

In 7th, 8th and 9th grades we had an annual class banquet for which the young ladies of our class prepared a wonderful dinner and served it in a dining room which was adjacent to the kitchen for their home economics classes. It was a special occasion for me, when in 9th grade I was asked to speak about my flying lessons. I proudly shared the experience of practicing stalls, forced landings, and tail spins, which were the most challenging parts of the flight course.

My father and I had both taken flying lessons at the Mt. Pleasant airport. I paid for my own with earnings from the summer hay field. During that spring of 1945, I logged enough hours to solo, but was not permitted to do so, because I was not yet 16 years of age. My father did solo, but we both quit flying when two air crashes resulted in severe injuries to our friends. In one case there was a serious back injury, in the other, a loss of limbs. Soon after we stopped flying, our flight instructor was found dead in a mountain air crash.

In 9th grade I was elected Student Body President of North Sanpete Jr. High. We had some special movies and dances at school, and I enjoyed playing on a junior high basketball team that was victorious over our rival teams in Fairview and Spring City Jr. High Schools.

Senior High School

As a Sophomore in high school, I was chosen, along with my friend Joe Jensen, to participate in an all state band. This band was scheduled to perform at the National Future Farmers of America Convention in Kansas City, Missouri. The convention was held in the Kansas City Municipal Auditorium in October of 1945. The picture below shows the all-state band in a practice session that was held at Snow College, in Ephraim, Utah, in late summer of 1945. A professor of music at Utah State University was our director.

Utah All State FFA Band

Our band traveled to Kansas City by train, sleeping in comfortable Pullman berths and dining in a formal setting with linen and silver. We also had a special car that was set up for section and individual practice. It was fun to prepare for a big time concert on a moving train. My clarinet and Joe's flute took on magic dimensions in this new environment.

When we arrived in Kansas City, we slept, along with hundreds of other FFA kids, in the hallways of the auditorium. Our beds were army cots, and we lined up at mealtime for catered food.

We were complimented and applauded for our concert program, and when it was finished we were asked to remain in our chairs while Mr. J. C. Penney came over to us, introduced himself, and moved among us, signing autographs.

After our concert we were called "men of leisure" and invited to tour the city the next morning. I was 15 years old at the time, but I was allowed to explore the streets of Kansas City, alone or with friends. I remember having my picture taken, and using my "spending money" to buy my father an electric shaver. On the last evening of the convention, the large audience of FFA kids was entertained by Mickey Rooney and other movie stars, as well as the famous Ray Noble orchestra.

Returning to school was special. The Sophomore Class at North Sanpete High School had been enriched when the graduates of Fairview and Spring City Junior High Schools were bussed in, giving us a combined senior high student body of approximately 165 students.

In the second half of my sophomore year, the spring of 1946, I obtained a driver license and began to take my father's Chrysler on occasional Saturday dates within the county. My week nights were consumed with school responsibilities, except for Friday, when students usually attended athletic events. In the fall the entire senior high student body was often bused to a nearby town to cheer for our team in an afternoon football game. In the winter we traveled on a bus to cheer at Friday evening basketball games. I was on the sophomore basketball team. We played in preliminary games before the varsity contests. Coach Miner kept me in uniform on the bench, after the sophomore preliminary, and used me occasionally in the varsity games.

In the summer of 1946 it was back to the grind and sweat of the hayfield, but weeknights were free. The family Chrysler was usually available for a Saturday night date. On one occasion I couldn't wait for the weekend, and after tossing hay bales onto trucks and wagons all day, I mustered the energy to ride my bicycle five miles each way to visit with a special young lady in a nearby town. But the pleasure of this mid-week adventure could not compare with what would happen on the weekend. There was nothing in the Sanpete Valley quite like the big Saturday night dance at Joyland, an open air dance floor on the main street in Moroni. Kids from every town in the county were there. We would cast off our work togs, dress up, and drive our cars from all points in the valley for the big night out. The girls were splendid in attractive summer dresses, while the boys wore dress slacks, oxfords and sports attire. We paid a small admission fee, got our hands stamped, passed through a doorway and walked onto a smooth cement dance floor surrounded by a high lattice fence. We huddled in groups, laughed, traded barbs, and exchanged pleasantries with the Revelers, a local swing band that was perched under an attractive band shell.

A few years earlier Mt. Pleasant had attracted these summer dance crowds with an open air facility named "Moonwinks," but in the mid to late 1940s, nothing in the Sanpete Valley could compare with a summer evening dance in Moroni. The carefree laughter, the smell of perfume, the whiff of alcohol and tobacco (here and there) the beautiful young ladies and the handsome young men, the occasional firecracker that went off someplace outside, the servicemen on furlough, the smart swing routines, the romantic slow dances, the beautiful starlit skies—all of this was part of the festive Joyland experience.

The best times for me, however, came in Salt Lake City. My father took me to the state basketball tournament each year when I was in Junior High School. That was great fun, but the crowning moment came in senior high when I could see a famous swing band at Jerry Jones' Rainbow Rendezvous. The Rainbow was a night spot in Salt Lake City where teens and adults could enjoy an evening of dancing to the music of big name bands. Stan Kenton, Benny Goodman, Harry James, Les Brown, Lionel Hampton, Buddy Rich, Mel Torme, Billy Eckstine, Gene Krupa, Tommy Dorsey, and many others came to the Rainbow. In Utah it was against the law to have liquor on the table in a night club, so the Rainbow experience was an evening with soft drinks and great entertainment---a wholesome experience that parents could feel reasonably comfortable about.

In the spring of 1947, I was able to spend a special evening at the Rainbow with a group of my friends from North Sanpete High School. We danced to the music of Charlie Spivak and returned to our homes in Mt. Pleasant and Spring City in the early morning hours.

In February of 1947 I was the prom master of the North Sanpete High School Junior Prom. Norma Jensen was the prom mistress (Appendix VII). The theme of our prom was "Daybreak." It was chosen not only because that was the title of a popular song of the day, but also because it symbolized the end of a horrible world war and the return of millions of brave veterans. It was to be a new day for the world, we said, and peace would replace war, and prosperity would replace the hopeless years of the Great Depression.

Day Break, Another New Day

Day break, another new day,
The mist on the meadow is drifting away.
For it's Day break, the sun's in the sky now
And flowers break through their blanket of dew.
Sunrise, how lovely it seems
To see from my window, a sky full of dreams.
As the white clouds sail on through the blue,
At Day break I day-dream of you.

From *Enn Ess Aitch*, the North Sanpete High School annual for 1947
The North Sanpete High School Junior Prom.

The center piece of the décor was a huge painting by famed Utah artist Max Blain. It was a magnificent mountain scene of a sunrise bursting forth through the Quaking Aspens. It covered a large portion of our east wall. Mr. Blain spent countless hours on this central part of the Junior promenade of 1947. I am grateful to this kind member of the NSHS faculty for his hard work.

Bright yellow streamers flowed out from the top of his picture. The streamers changed to light orange, then light blue, culminating in sky blue at the outer reaches of the hall. I spent many hours with my friends, hanging streamers and making the preparations for the big event. (Appendix VII)

Soon after the prom there was new excitement. In March of 1947, the University of Utah basketball team won the National Invitational Tournament. Arnold Ferrin, Vern Gardner, Leon Watson, Fred Sheffield, and Wat Misaka were the starting five. They defeated Adolph Rupp's famous Kentucky Wildcats. The Wildcats had all-American Ralph Beard, Alex Groza, Wah Wah Jones, and other famous players of the day. I heard the game on the radio, and I was so excited that I could hardly sleep that night.

The next morning I went to school chattering with my buddies about how the Utah Utes had won the national championship in basketball. Unlike basketball teams of today, the players were home grown stars who were, with one exception, recruited from Utah high schools. As we sat down to respond to roll call in our early morning seminary class, I whispered to Richard Hansen and Ted Kay. "The Utes are flying home this morning. They will arrive at the Salt Lake City airport at 10:30 am. We've got to be there. Let's go!" That was all it took. The three of us walked out of morning seminary class, stood in front of our high school and stopped a ton-and-a-half truck. The driver asked what we wanted, and I explained that the Utes had won the national championship in basketball and we wanted to be part of the celebration when they arrived at the Salt Lake airport in a couple of hours. The driver said "Okay, hop in the back."

It was a chilly mid-March morning. We had the sum total of fifteen cents, but we enthusiastically jumped into the back of the big truck, pulled our jackets over our heads and rode over one hundred miles as the wind whipped our clothing and whistled around us. It was obvious that the two men who were up in the warm cab were headed toward Salt Lake City, but they were certainly kind and thoughtful in making a circuitous route directly to the airport.

We arrived in time to greet the victorious Utes. There was a huge crowd and we participated in an airport pep rally. Vern Gardner got a special welcome as he had been named the most valuable player of the NIT. He was asked to stand on top of a huge fire engine and lead a victory procession into the city. Behind the fire engine came the rest of the team, each sitting on top of the back seats of handsome convertible automobiles. Students from the university gave us a ride and we became a part of the procession, following quite closely behind the team.

With fire bells clanging, the procession headed toward the city where we participated in a Salt Lake version of a ticker tape parade. It happened that 1947 was the centennial year for the State of Utah. In the downtown rally, the Governor, the Mayor of Salt Lake City, University officials, cheer leaders, a pep band, and students and people from various parts of the state celebrated a glorious occasion. I knew then that this was a once-in-a-lifetime experience, and I was fortunate to be there with my friends.

When the festivities ended downtown, the team went up to the University campus to hold another rally in Kingsbury Hall. At this juncture Richard, Ted and I bought a loaf of bread and wolfed it down with a little water from a public drinking fountain. Our money was now gone and we needed a ride back to Mt. Pleasant. We walked back to the highway, and fortunately we were able to "hitch" a ride with a friend from Fairview. We were once again in a large truck, but this time our friend allowed us to crowd together in the warm cab.

I shared the entire story with my father that evening. He complimented me for being creative and resourceful. He said he was proud of me. But next day the principal of North Sanpete High called him and asked him for a note before I could be admitted back in school. My father,

Joseph A. Cadet of the Month at South High

who was no longer Superintendent of Schools, would not supply the note. I explained to my principal that I did not intend to violate school rules, but if I had worked through channels and negotiated for transportation, we could never have been able to make the trip. I also explained that it was not a malicious act, that I had never been in trouble at school, and that I was willing to do anything to be part of that epic moment in the history of our state—and I naively added, I was not sorry, and under the same circumstances I would do it again.

My principal admitted me and my friends back in school without notes, but in my case, there were consequences. The balance of my school year was uncomfortable and I opted to find a new school for my senior year (Appendix III).

In the fall of 1947 I chose to live with my paternal grandmother, Hannah Christensen Bagnall, in Salt Lake City, where I enrolled in South High School. My grandmother was diabetic. She was losing her eyesight. At this time of her life she needed me to help her with insulin injections, to read to her, and to take her with me to school programs, to church, and other places. I needed her as well. We lived in the Waldorf Apartments, owned by Armont Willardsen, the director of South High School's famous 211-voice a cappella choir. I was proudly a member of that choir. We performed as the model choir at a music educators' convention for the State of Utah. If that invitation did not confirm the quality of our group, our reputation was enhanced when the conductor of the Mormon Tabernacle Choir attended our practice sessions a few times. The following year our choir traveled to Pasadena, California, where it performed at the National Music Educators Conference and conducted clinics. After the official business was complete, choir members toured San Francisco (Appendix IV).

It was a challenge to come from a senior high school with 165 students to a new school with over 2400 students. When I started at South, I didn't know anyone in the school. Fortunately I soon made new friends.

I was chosen South High ROTC Cadet of the Month for September 1947. Given the size of the battalion and the fact that it was my first month at the new school, it was certainly not expected, but it was a pleasant surprise!

My classes at South were all well taught, and I was a receptive and industrious student. I thoroughly enjoyed Armont Willardsen's a cappella class, and my English and math classes. I also have fond memories of Mr. Garrish in chemistry and Mrs. Christensen in American Problems.

Mrs. Christensen asked me to represent South High in a *Deseret News* Roundtable discussion. Four students were chosen to participate: one from East, West, South, and Granite High Schools, respectively. A faded copy of the *Deseret News* account of the roundtable is all that can be retrieved over sixty years later. It is included in this book (Appendix V).

Joseph A. Bagnall Class of 1948
South High School Salt Lake City, Utah

While I had been able to play on the athletic teams at North Sanpete High, at South High I had to find a new way to engage my interest in sports. I decided to work as a sports reporter. My work on the *South High Scribe* and the ROTC drill team were counted as my extracurricular activities at South. When they were combined with academic points garnered in the classroom, they helped earn me a place at the Honors and Awards Banquet. That was a nice way to end my senior year.

Chapter Three: College Days

The summer before I attended the University of Utah, I worked in a warehouse in Salt Lake City. In the fall of 1948 I enrolled at the University, but I dropped my classes half-way through the fall semester with the intention of making my real start in the spring. I took classes at the University in the spring of 1949 lived with my grandmother, and worked as a sports reporter on *The Daily Utah Chronicle*, the student newspaper at the University.

I value my experience as a reporter on "the Chronie." I covered many football and basketball games, The highlight of my freshman year was writing the feature story of the retiring of All-American Vern Gardner's No 33 basketball jersey. The article was published on May 11, 1949 (Appendix VI).

Three staffers on the *Daily Utah Chronicle*
Left to Right: Joe Bagnall, Bob Muir, and Clint Barber Photo Credit: The *Utonian*, 1949.

But it was not until the fall of 1949 that I got into the full swing of college life. I pledged to Pi Kappa Alpha fraternity and since my Aunt Jean, father's adopted sister, could help my grandmother, I moved to the fraternity house on campus. My freshman studies were interrupted with card games, big band rehearsals, parties with sorority girls, and anything else that happened to be going on in the house. My fraternity brothers referred to one another as left wing or right wing. Lefties were party animals who would "chug-a-lug" beer, smoke cigarettes and make the academic experience at college secondary to having the most fun possible. I was the designated driver when my "leftie" friends went to a "watering hole" for chug-a-lug rounds. I would join in the singing, sip a soft drink, and watched my brothers down a bottle of beer with each round. They were a hopeless but loveable bunch when they piled into the car to go back to the house.

I had a wonderful time in the fraternity, mixing with all kinds, but I managed to remain a right winger socially, so when I was interviewed for Mormon missionary service in June 1950, I could answer the hard questions with a straight face.

My fraternity brothers were leaders in campus organizations and in athletics. In spite of the challenges of initiation and the indignities that were heaped upon pledges, I was fortunate to have the advantage of this splendid support group. The fraternity experience was a positive one for me. The University of Utah will always be a special place for me as well.

In the spring of 1950 I was called to serve a mission for the Church of Jesus Christ of Latter-day Saints. I accepted the call and served in Henryetta, Oklahoma, Poplar Bluff, Missouri, and Independence, Missouri. I worked hard, and achieved most of my missionary goals. It seems, however, that I had difficulty conforming to the narrow focus and the strict constraints of missionary life. I had spent my entire youth in a strict environment, surrendering my childhood to the lot of a ranch hand. I had played the role of a dutiful son of a Mormon church official and Superintendent of Schools and neglected my basic need to express a few of my own thoughts and feelings. I had achieved all the priesthood awards, worked through the ranks of scouting, and I felt saturated with good things carried to an extreme. I was unhappy, and confused. I lost weight, became sick and was sent home to recover. At this time I had about six months of weekly outpatient psychotherapy. I was given an honorable release from my mission, and I have resumed life successfully, since that time, in more moderate settings and more balanced environments.

In 1951 my father responded to a call to operate the Southern California Regional Welfare Ranch of the Church of Jesus Christ of Latter-day Saints. I went with my parents to our new ranch home in Perris, California. Originally this ranch was developed as an elegant retreat for Louis B. Mayer of Metro Goldwyn Mayer movie fame. It had a race track and splendid accommodations for Mayer's guests and his horses. When the LDS Church bought this property, it was converted into a traditional ranch with cattle, chickens, hogs, alfalfa, and row crops of various kinds. Five or six families lived on the ranch to ensure rational continuity, but the bulk of the labor was supplied by LDS church members of the Southern California region. Each Saturday, 50 to 100 eager workers would arrive to hoe or harvest their special stake welfare project. For example, a Long Beach stake might be raising watermelons, and a San Diego stake might be raising potatoes. On the designated Saturday, when it was time for the San Diego stake to weed their potatoes, the ranch awakened to the din of honking automobiles, laughter, and the happy sounds of volunteer workers. And to what end was all this activity focused? This was an integral part of the vast church welfare system, conceived to provide for the needs of the Mormon poor.

For a few months I painted buildings on the welfare ranch and attended nearby Riverside City College. After one semester, I moved to Los Angeles, worked as an apprentice proof reader on *The Los Angeles Times* and attended Los Angeles City College.

After about six months on the *Times*, I went over to *The Los Angeles Herald Express* to work as a copy boy. Each day I raced across town in my 1948 Mercury Convertible and picked up the latest editions of *The Los Angeles Times, The Los Angeles Daily News,* and *The Los Angeles Examiner,* and brought them back to *The Herald Express.* Since each paper had at least three editions daily, I was constantly on the go, making certain that our competitor's "scoops" were in the hands of the *Herald* rewrite men as soon as they broke. In addition I was a general factotum for the news room, running back pictures from famous trials and big news events. I did this work with enthusiasm because the sports editor gave me the opportunity to cover some high school basketball, and the editorial staff allowed me to review a few books for the *Herald* editorial page (Appendix VII).

Chapter Four: Salad Years

In 1953 I married Phyllis Luck, and my newspaper carried a nice article under the headline, "Wedding Bells for Herald Man." Soon thereafter I realized that I wanted to pursue a career in education so I combined a new work assignment at the Los Angeles Public Library with upper division studies at California State University at Los Angeles. In the spring of 1955, I graduated with a Bachelor of Arts in Elementary Education and a lifetime California teaching credential. I was immediately hired as a fifth grade teacher in the newly opened La Rosa Elementary School in the Temple City Unified School District, and the faculty chose me to represent La Rosa Elementary in the Temple City Education Association.

Dabbling in Politics

It had been my good fortune to serve as the President of the Greater Arcadia Stevenson for President Club in 1956. After the national election of that year, I received an invitation to a special reception to honor Senator John F. Kennedy at the Biltmore Hotel in Los Angeles. Ostensibly the occasion was for Dore Schary, a Hollywood movie producer, to present a plaque to the young Senator for narrating a film that aired in the 1956 Democratic convention titled "The Pursuit of Happiness." But it seems the real reason for the reception was an attempt by JFK handlers to explore a presidential run.

It was special to watch Kennedy mingle enthusiastically with the Hollywood crowd and about 50 Democratic Party leaders, Governor Edmund G. (Pat) Brown among them. I had a brief conversation with JFK, asked him to make a presidential run in 1960, and told him I would do my part to help him in the effort. He thanked me for my interest and support, but said that he wasn't considering it at that time. I signed his guest list and left the meeting hoping he would run.

Soon thereafter there was a nice letter thanking me for my "generous offer of support" and an autographed 8 X 10 photograph in my mailbox. He also sent Christmas cards for the next two years. All of these things are mounted in a large, handsome frame in my study.

After two delightful years as an elementary teacher and part time study at Cal State LA, I was able to take leave of my work responsibilities to engage in two semesters of full time study for my Masters Degree. I am deeply grateful to my parents for partial financial assistance at that time. Our family of five lived on a budget of $200 per month.

Research for graduate seminar papers in the late 1950s was done without copying machines. It was necessary to spend hours in the library, copying notes on 4 x 6 cards that I carried in a shoe box. It was an extensive process to read and transfer information by hand. The alternative was to check out stacks of books and do the same tedious work at home. My research papers were typed on a typewriter. Mistakes had to be taken out with a rubber eraser and *single* copies were made by inserting two sheets of paper in the typewriter with a carbon sheet between them. If I needed multiple copies it was necessary to type the material on a ditto master or a mimeograph stencil, and then go back to school and attach the master, or the stencil, to a drum on a machine that I turned by hand. The spell checker of that day was a hard copy dictionary. Copying machines, computers and the internet have given students of the 21st Century enormous advantages in research.

After parking in a nearby dirt lot, I spent much of my research time at the Los Angeles Public Library The library was an imposing structure in the world of that time. There is now a huge skyscraper where I used to park, and the library is now an afterthought, dwarfed under the towering buildings that surround it.

After my year of full time study, I returned to La Rosa Elementary School for one more year. Simultaneously I finished the final requirements for a Masters Degree in history with a minor in political science. The big hurdle was taking comprehensive essay examinations in four fields of history----United States to 1877, United States Since 1877, Western America, and Modern Europe. I also earned lifetime California teaching credentials on the general secondary and community college levels.

In 1959 I was hired as a teacher of history, geography, and journalism, and as adviser to *The Galleon*, a weekly student newspaper at Monterey High School. In the evenings I served as an adjunct in American history at Monterey Peninsula College.

In my first semester at Monterey High, David Matt, an English instructor, accompanied me and my *Galleon* staffers to a journalism conference at Stanford University. We traveled by bus and had a wonderful time.

Aware of the fact that Alexander Kerensky, Prime Minister of the provisional government of Russia, was a resident scholar at Stanford's Library on War, Peace, and Revolution, David and I decided to try to get an interview with him. It was Saturday morning so Kerensky was at his apartment on campus. We knocked on his door and he greeted us in robe and slippers. We identified ourselves as visiting journalists on campus and requested a brief interview with him. He very graciously invited us in and granted us a 20 minute interview in which he described the difficulties of his interim government in Russia, between Czarist rule and the Communist takeover. One of the best parts of his account was his escape from Russia disguised as a woman. Characterizing the Soviet regime as the most reactionary in the world, he correctly predicted it would fail. The interview, while brief, was a most exciting experience!

In the spring of 1960, on a Sunday evening, I was marking student papers when the telephone rang. I answered and a voice said "Hello, this is Senator Kennedy." I expected I would hear from him as I had left a note in his box at his Pebble Beach hotel, where he and Jackie were resting after a hard fought victory in the Oregon primary. My note contained a congratulatory statement on victory in Oregon, a reminder that I was one of his earliest endorsers for a presidential run, and a simple request to allow my student reporters from the Monterey High *Galleon* to attend any press conference that he might hold on the Monterey Peninsula. He explained that there would not be a press conference during his stay, but if he had planned one, our reporters would certainly have been included.

During this same year Linden Leavitt, Dean of the evening division at Monterey Peninsula College, scheduled and sponsored the most outstanding array of community events I have ever seen. Eleanor Roosevelt, Martin Luther King, Jr. and former Prime Minister Clement Atlee were part of his evening lecture series. (A couple of my *Galleon* reporters were able to sit in on press conferences held by Roosevelt and Atlee). In addition to this magnificent evening lecture series, he organized

The Bagnall family in 1964. Left to Right **Top**: Pamela and Nancy Jo, **Middle:** Phyllis and Joseph A., **Bottom** Melanie and Joseph M. Nancy Jo served as President of the Student Body at Wilshire Jr. High School and won a Kiwanis Award. Later on Pamela served as Vice President at Wilshire Jr. High. Phyllis served as President of Faculty Wives at Fullerton College.

Great Book discussion groups, seminar luncheons and many other notable activities. His stellar work in community service and continuing education inspired my own life-time career goals.

After two years on the Monterey Peninsula, I decided to return to Southern California to study for my doctorate in history. Taking a position at Millikan High School in Long Beach, I spent the next three years studying part-time in the evening division at the University of Southern California.

In 1964, I was hired for a full time position in the Social Science division at Fullerton College (See Foreword). I taught classes in my major, which was American history, and my minor, which was political science.

In 1965 I published a book titled *Depression Dialogue: An Anthology of Representative Political Dialogue of the Depression Decade*. It was useful in my classroom and can be found in libraries of colleges and universities across America today (Appendix X).

In extracurricular activities I served as foreign student adviser. On April 22, 1968 the foreign students of Fullerton College hosted foreign student organizations from nine other community colleges in a gala International Day celebration. Events of the day included: a full-length movie on the Life of Albert Schweitzer, a karate demonstration, A Radio Telesymposium in which radio talk show host, Joel Spivak, brought his three hour radio program to campus. Spivak sat on stage, as moderator, in the 500 seat campus theatre, with a foreign student panel and me. We, in turn, were hooked, via telephone, with Senators Robert F. Kennedy of New York, Thomas Kuchel of California, and John Tower of Texas. Questions were posed by the panel to the Senators on two topics: Red China and Vietnam. Questions were next taken from students from the audience who lined up and participated, on microphones placed in the aisles, and finally people called in from the vast Southern California radio audience with questions. This was a communication coup that involved foreign students from nine other campuses, a portion of our own student body, a few townsmen, and a large Southern California radio audience. The energy at this event was awesome. It was special to extend the boundaries of our International Day far beyond the confines of our college campus. Our student newspaper covered the event with a banner headline (Appendix VIII).

After the three hour broadcast, Fullerton College international students played Chaffey College international students in a soccer game. The final event of International Day was a dance in the Fullerton College Student Center featuring the music of the Disneyland Hotel swing band.

Chapter Five: My Epiphany

The excitement of International Day and the aforementioned example of Dean Linden Leavitt, led me to change my career goals. I dropped the Ph.D. program in history at USC in favor of an Ed.D. program at UCLA. From this point on my goal was to become a community service and continuing education administrator in the tradition of Linden Leavitt.

When I started my classes in 1968, the UCLA campus was in turmoil with student protests against the Vietnam War. Some students would pile furniture and debris around the entrance to the chancellor's office. Others would sit in the middle of the street and block traffic on Wilshire Blvd. Sometimes the protesters would hold mass rallies on campus, and sometimes they would just sit around in large groups smoking "pot."

One of the tragic moments in this period happened late at night, as I was driving home from UCLA. My radio was tuned in to hear the results of the California Primary. The news reporter described the Kennedy victory celebration, and almost in the same breath, he reported that Senator Robert F. Kennedy had been shot.

Fortunately for graduate students, most of the campus turmoil at UCLA was taking place in the daytime. When I arrived for my evening classes the environment was more settled and serious. My classes were filled with mature students whose focus was not only on educational issues, but also on the serious political issues of the day. Many of us were highly critical of President Johnson and his foreign policy, but it seems we were more thoughtful and less inclined to support the direct action strategies of some of the younger set. We also identified with that portion of the student body who held to campus traditions. In this realm the fantastic John Wooden and his UCLA basketball team were making national headlines. Year after year, to the sum of ten, the UCLA Bruins won the national championship. This helped to keep some semblance of the traditional college atmosphere in place.

My classes at UCLA were challenging. I would finish my work day at Fullerton College and drive to the UCLA campus, inching along the freeway in rush hour traffic with a sandwich and a reel to reel tape recorder on the seat. I would record the material I needed to study before hand, and my "study tapes" were always an essential part of the long drive to campus. Over a four year period, this routine would eventually prepare me to gain an administrative position in the nationally acclaimed continuing education program at Santa Barbara City College.

At City College, I would write a doctoral dissertation describing the Santa Barbara City College program. Its title would be *The Development and Maintenance of a Continuing Education Program at the Community College Level.* But of more immediate concern was my field project for my doctoral program-----the founding of a student organization at Fullerton College called The Center for the Study of the Future of Man. The inspiration for this Fullerton College Center came from the scholars at the Center for the Study of Democratic Institutions in Santa Barbara, whom I came to know and appreciate as a result of an event in the late 1960s. In 1968 I had published a college supplementary reader titled *President John F. Kennedy: A Grand and Global Alliance: The Summons to World Peace through World Law* (Appendix X). I sent the fellows at the Santa Barbara Center a copy of my book and asked if I could bring students from my classes at Fullerton to discuss the content of the Kennedy reader with them. Vice President Frank K. Kelly invited us to the center where Robert Hutchins, Harry Ashmore and other scholars dialogued with my students. An account of the visit was published on the back cover of *The Center Magazine.*

But more importantly, I became sensitive to the writings and the concerns of the fellows at the Center for the Study of Democratic Institutions. In setting up our Fullerton Center, I made certain that our areas of study would reflect the vital concerns I had heard in Santa Barbara.

Clearing the pathway for my field project was not easy. First, I simultaneously introduced the idea of a Fullerton College Center to Dr. John Casey, President of Fullerton College and to Dr. Clarence Fielstra, Chairman of my doctoral committee at UCLA. I explained that a Center for the Study of the Future of Man could have its basic roots in **a special section of the college library** with books and articles dedicated to the development of survival perspectives. Students could go there to find books on nuclear issues, environmental concerns, ethnic and poverty issues, and strategies for world peace. **Second,** the Center could build up a strong student membership and charge a small fee in order to finance a student forum on survival issues, and **Third,** the Center should promote rational dialogue and gradual reforms in a period where colleges and universities were experiencing student tirades, student riots, disorder, campus violence and the destruction of school property.

Dr. Casey enthusiastically helped me set up an advisory board for our Fullerton Center. The Board included many prominent faculty members and a Dean of Instruction. We then began to implement the ideas I had presented.

The Center organization soon grew to over 500 student members. Norman Cousins, the distinguished editor of *Saturday Review,* came to campus and gave a dedicatory address which focused on the quest for world peace. This was followed by an address on environmental concerns by Stewart Udall, Secretary of the Interior in the Kennedy and Johnson administrations. Other speakers in the Center forum were Frank K. Kelly, Vice President of the Center for the Study of Democratic Institutions, Richard Buffum, columnist for the Orange County Edition of the

Los Angeles Times, and President John Casey of our own Fullerton College. Students listened thoughtfully and engaged in productive discussions.

When the Nixon administration ordered the bombing of Cambodia, every community college in the state of California, with the exception of Fullerton College, had to close due to violent student protests. The Center cooperated with the college administration and other groups on campus to set up a speakers' platform where students and faculty could sign up to stand before huge crowds and voice their opinions on foreign policy and the Vietnam War. The speeches went on throughout the day, and so did our classes. Rational dialogue and gradual reform were Center hallmarks and this approach was viewed with wide favor. Richard Buffum praised the Center in three separate columns in the *Los Angeles Times*. An Orange County reporter for the *Times* also wrote a nice feature article about our work.

Chapter Six: The Santa Barbara Years, 1970-1982

By 1970 a position as Assistant Dean opened in the Continuing Education Division at Santa Barbara City College. I applied for it and got the job. However, the Superintendent-President looked at my dearth of administrative experience and asked me to serve a year as a coordinator. After one year I became Assistant Dean.

In my first year I worked with Dean Selmer O. (Sam) Wake to hone my skills as supervisor of about 85 instructors and focus my thoughts on a vast array of administrative challenges. I soon became a vital cog in the national pace-setting Santa Barbara City College Continuing Education Division. Our program boasted over 33,000 individual enrollments annually. My areas of supervision were World National and Local Affairs, Philosophy and Humanities, Science, Music, English as a Second Language, Basic (Adult) Education, Santa Barbara City College Adult Evening High School, Continuing Education Buildings and Grounds, and the Student Body Account.

In addition to about 85 vital, well attended classes in my areas of supervision, I developed at least four community lecture series each semester. Some prominent speakers featured in these series were: Robert M. Hutchins, Senator Wayne Morse, Dr. Jack Peltason, and others, on the topic "Do We Need a New U. S. Constitution?" Dr. Edward Teller, Amory Lovins, Secretary of Interior Stewart Udall, Roger Billings, Ralph Nader, and others on alternative energy sources; Ruth Carter Stapleton (sister of President Carter) on the power of love; Attorney General Ramsey Clark and Congressman Barry Goldwater, Jr., as speakers on the Bicentennial of the American Revolution; Dr. David P. Gardner, President of the University of Utah and later Chancellor of the University of California system, on educational issues, and Nan Waterman, President of Common Cause, on national issues of the day.

Prominent lecturers that were scheduled in World National and Local Affairs were: **Governors** E.G. (Pat) Brown of California, Tom McCall of Oregon, Scott Matheson of Utah, and Robert F. List of Nevada; **Senators** Eugene McCarthy of Minnesota, Mark Hatfield of

Oregon, and George McGovern, of South Dakota. **Congresswoman** Patsy Mink also gave an address.

James Macgregor Burns, Henry Steele Commager and Arthur Schlessinger, Jr., were among the distinguished scholars who participated, as well as Harry Ashmore, Pulitzer Prize journalist, Frances Moore Lappe, Hugh Downs, Robert F. Kennedy, Jr., Norman Cousins, Raghavan Iyer, and Clifton Fadiman.

Distinguished economists who lectured for our division were: Robert L. Heilbroner, Rexford G. Tugwell, E. F. Schumacher, Paul Erdman, Stanley Sheinbaum, and Walter Mead.

In the area of science I scheduled Barry Commoner on energy and environment, Dr. Martin Cline on biogenetic engineering, Dr. Paul Ehrlich on the population explosion, Dr. Howard Jarvik on the artificial heart, Wesley Marx on *The Frail Ocean*, Dr. Roderick Nash on preserving wilderness, Dr. Norman Rassmussen, Chairperson of Nuclear Science at MIT, on nuclear energy, Dr. Jonas Salk on survival issues, Dr. Mario Molina, Nobel Prize scientist and co-discoverer of ozone depletion, on ozone depletion, G. Harry Stine on the space shuttle, Dr. Garret Hardin on the lifeboat ethic, Alexander Comfort on aging, and Dr. Paul Saltman on biogenetic engineering.

For special lectures in the Humanities I brought in world famous psychologists Carl Rogers and Albert Ellis. Other speakers were Dr. Hardin Branch, past president of the American Psychiatric Association, who spoke on societal issues and Leonard Weinglass, who spoke on privacy and civil rights.

In music programming I scheduled a lecture on opera by Dr. Jan Popper and performances by the L.A. Jazz Choir, The Roger Wagner Chorale, The Four Freshmen, the Shelley Manne Trio, Buddy Childers, and the Cal State jazz ensembles from the universities at Northridge and Los Angeles. In addition I started the Santa Barbara City College Night Band. The highlight of this performing group was an evening concert featuring Ann Richards, a singer from the Stan Kenton Band, as guest vocalist.

January 30, 1982, was the 100th anniversary of the birth of Franklin D. Roosevelt. To commemorate this day I scheduled former Congressman and eldest son of FDR, James Roosevelt, to give a centenary address. James was nearly always at his father's side, grasping steadfastly to his arm, holding him and guiding him, as he shuffled and swayed with ten pounds of steel locked onto his crippled legs.

On his fourth inauguration day, James stood behind his father, witnessing a frail, infirm man, struggling to muster his strength for a five minute inaugural address. James was in uniform, having been called from his post in WW II. It was at this time that FDR passed his ring to James, honoring a Roosevelt tradition that it should go to the eldest son.

James was our dinner guest before his address. At that time, he passed FDR's ring around to a few school officials and I was privileged to handle it for a moment. After dinner James' address was filled with firsthand accounts of the heroic Roosevelt years.

Public lectures and performances had been the public face--the capstone--over approximately

85 well attended classes in all of my program areas. It was a great blessing to be able to tap the rich pool of talent that was available from the faculties of Santa Barbara City College and the University of California at Santa Barbara—and then there were the resident scholars at the Center for the Study of Democratic Institutions. The Center furnished not only great speakers, but also my programming ally, Vice President Frank K. Kelly. Frank and I teamed up to bring many of the Fellows at the Center into my public events at Santa Barbara City College. We also issued simultaneous invitations to nationally prominent speakers in World, National, and Local Affairs. Distinguished national leaders would receive a dual invitation to spend the day in dialogue with distinguished scholars at the Center, and in the evening they were asked to give a lecture to a Santa Barbara community audience under the auspices of Santa Barbara City College. As an added incentive for prospective speakers, the Center dialogues were published in the *Center Magazine,* and given wide distribution among the intellectual elite, nationally.

Frank K. Kelly was a good friend. His contributions to the Center, to the Santa Barbara community, and to national thought, were enormous (Appendix XII). He was also personally significant to me--- a central figure in my professional life.

Another person who loomed large with me was Paul Relis. He was the leader at the Santa Barbara Community Environmental Council. I worked with Paul to develop many classes that reflected environmental concerns. We also developed an ongoing public lecture series titled The American Dream and the City of Man.

In 1973, Dr. Martin Bobgan, longtime Assistant Dean in the continuing education program, succeeded Sam Wake as Dean of Continuing Education. He restructured the division in a very effective way. He hired two talented coordinators to program his own areas of supervision. Marian Johnson and Ellen Downing worked very effectively with him in developing and expanding important areas of his program. The Bobgan-Downing team was spectacular in the development of a lecture series in the field of psychology titled Mind and Supermind. As of this writing (2009) the series remains the all-time leader in terms of audience size and longevity. Dr. Bobgan and Ellen Downing have long since retired, but Mind and Supermind, I am told, is still running strong.

Dr. Bobgan asked me to deliver a keynote address "Providing Comprehensive Education for California Adults in the 1980s" at the statewide conference of The California Community Services Association and The California Community College Continuing Education Association, held April 25-27, 1979, at Asilomar, California. There were three keynoters. I was proud to represent and describe the Santa Barbara City College Continuing Education program. There was much interest and many questions after my address.

My twelve years at Santa Barbara City College were challenging in the extreme. From 1970-1973, in addition to my work in the Continuing Education Division, I opted to finish my doctorate at UCLA. I completed that heavy task successfully, while also co-authoring a history book that was published in 1973. After Dr. Bobgan became Dean, in addition to the vast array of responsibilities mentioned earlier, I was assigned to supervise the office staff and the audio visual department. My work day began at 10 am and ended when I had locked the office down and taken an audio visual worker home. I usually pulled into my own driveway after 10 pm. For twelve long years my time and energy were focused on work and career, and my family paid a heavy price. After over a quarter of a century my marriage ended in divorce.

Chapter Seven: New Directions

After 27 years in the field of education, I opted for an early retirement, married my secretary, Naomi Blasjo, and we moved back to the Chester ranch in Utah. I had spent the past two summer vacations in Utah painting and fixing up the ranch house, so after a honeymoon on the Monterey Peninsula and in San Francisco, we moved into our country home in the latter part of July, 1982.

Joseph and Naomi Bagnall in 1982

The early ranch days were relatively carefree. The ranch was leased to a cattle man. I helped my father oversee the property and spent some happy days driving steel posts and doing some heavy fencing around the grassland pastures.

When winter came we rented an apartment in Salt Lake City, where I worked as a substitute teacher in a number of Salt Lake City high schools. I also volunteered at a radio station where I wrote and narrated a script on JFK's foreign policy that was aired on his birthday. Later I arranged to have the program uplinked to a satellite where it went out in a soft feed to hundreds of National Public Radio stations. A number of them aired the program. At this juncture, my daughter, Melanie, presented the idea of making a television documentary utilizing my JFK script, to her employer, Richard Dennison. Mr. Dennison assumed the role of Executive Producer for the resultant television documentary.

Gene Minshall, a talented Utah film maker, worked with me to piece together footage from the JFK library, score the production, and film Robert Vaughn, the narrator, in his on camera sequences. Our half hour documentary titled "John F. Kennedy's Lost Pathway to Peace," aired on TBS, the SuperStation and on KCET, the Los Angeles PBS affiliate, on the 70th anniversary of JFK's birth. It has also aired on UCSD TV, KOCT Oceanside TV, and Palomar College TV.

On December 10, 1984, I was in the delivery room at Holy Cross Hospital in Salt Lake City, when Naomi gave birth to Ashley Jo Bagnall, our first and only child (Appendix XIII). She was a beautiful baby who made our last few months in Utah very happy.

Naomi had made careful preparations for the arrival of our new family member. She read Dr. Benjamin Spock's book on infant and child care, and she purchased a basinet, numerous infant toys, and a used crib, which she sanded and repainted. Over the crib she hung an attractive mobile. It seemed that she had anticipated everything when we brought our little girl home.

When Ashley was a toddler, Naomi posted large letters at baby-eye-level at different spots in the room. When Ashley toddled to one area, mother would point and say "A," in another area she would point and say "B," and another and say "C," etc. As a result, at age 19 months Ashley knew her ABCs. She was also able to spell dozens of words at age 3½. I remember playing games with her where mom and dad would spell words and Ashley would say the word.

When she entered kindergarten, Ashley was reading simple children's books (new material) effortlessly, but her mother didn't end her involvement there. Naomi held Ashley on her lap as she read the entire *Little House on the Prairie* series in first grade. In her early elementary years she also read the entire *Wizard of Oz* series, as well as books by Beverly Cleary, E. B. White, and a few on Greek mythology. In later Elementary years she read *The Chronicles of Narnia* series and other "chapter books." In the middle school years they sat side by side devouring James Herriot books. Both Ashley and I are deeply grateful to Naomi. She not only was a superb mother, but she has also been a wonderful wife.

It is instructive to note that immediately following high school graduation, Naomi served as a medical missionary. She was part of a group called Amigos de las Americas that went to a small village in Guatemala and gave basic immunizations to residents of that area. Her next personal milestone came when she graduated from Santa Barbara City College and was honored at commencement as "The Outstanding Woman Student of the Class of 1977." In 1978 she was an "au pair" girl living with a French family in a suburb of Paris. At that time she studied French at a school in Paris as well.

She still actively pursues her study of languages. For many years she and I were lulled to sleep with her English vocabulary tapes playing in the background. When she is not involved with her work at Wedbush Morgan Securities, or with her family and friends, she is poring over study materials in Spanish or Italian.

Her secondary hobby is mathematics. She has spent many hours in classes and labs at MiraCosta College, thoroughly enjoying herself in the process. Math studies, like language studies, are for self improvement and life enrichment only.

Meanwhile, back to Salt Lake City in 1984---the dreams of retirement in the country were shattered by the realities of the experience. Naomi was a Santa Barbara lady who tried her best to adapt to numerous new challenges. She was a wonderful helpmate on the Chester ranch, but she was more at home in Salt Lake City, where we spent some happy hours with Arthur Lee Monson, a Mt. Pleasant friend who was the Salt Lake County Treasurer. We also spent happy hours with filmmaker Gene Minshall and his wife Pam. Gene and I worked in his editing studio, traveled to New York to film Robert Vaughn, to Santa Barbara to share our finished film with Frank K. Kelly and others, and to Los Angeles to share our film with Norman Cousins at UCLA.

After three years in Utah, Naomi and I assessed our situation. By 1985 it was clear that we both yearned for California. We missed the ethnic diversity and the cosmopolitan environment of Santa Barbara. We had both experienced culture shock, and for my part, I desperately needed to get back into an educational setting. We therefore traveled to Carlsbad, California, to respond to a teaching opportunity at Army Navy Academy. I interviewed and was hired as Chairman of the Social Science Department for the coming academic year.

The Army Navy Academy was a private military school, located on the Carlsbad beach, offering grades 7 through 12 to prospective cadets from affluent families. In my eleven years at the Academy I saw cadets picked up by their respective families in high style. On one occasion a helicopter landed on the football field, on another, cadets swam out to board the family yacht, and then there was the cadet who rode home to San Francisco in a limousine.

Army Navy Academy was a good fit for me at that time. I was receiving a retirement check from the California State Retirement System and was therefore ineligible for full time work in public schools, colleges and universities. I could work full time, however, at this fine private school, and part time hourly in the local community college. I therefore spent the next eleven years, 1985-1996 as a full time employee at Army and Navy Academy and a part time-hourly adjunct in the evening division at Mira Costa College in Oceanside.

Army Navy Academy was an ideal place to teach adolescents. The Commandant would handle serious discipline problems so effectively that I did not have to deal with secondary problems and full attention could be given to subject matter. Classes were small, running to a high of perhaps 15. In this environment it was possible to perform miracles in the classroom. Students who had failed miserably in other educational settings would blossom and qualify for entrance, many with academic scholarships, into fine colleges and universities. We also competed in a league of private schools in football, basketball, baseball, swimming, water polo, rifle team, and other sports. Social activities on campus included numerous dances on campus along with an annual military ball.

I left my mark on the Academy in two important ways. I started the honors and advanced placement courses in social science and the annual trip to Harvard Model Congress. Harvard Model Congress was a mock Congress sponsored by Harvard University, and it was held annually in Boston in February. The model congress was composed of over 500 high school students, mostly from schools located in the eastern region of the United States. Students who participated were assigned the identities of real Congressmen and Senators. Participants were expected to carry out committee assignments, draft legislation, and debate in a manner that was reflective of the philosophy and commitment of the real political figure they were impersonating. Some students were also designated lobbyists and one student was chosen president. The ultimate objective in this marvelous four day laboratory in American government was to get a bill passed and signed by the president.

The challenges connected with the preparation and the logistics of this annual trip were overshadowed by the euphoria and the adventure associated with the event. About 15 Army and Navy cadets went each year. A few of them won awards each time I took them. I shared the pleasure of their achievements and took special pride in the fact that we were the only school in California ever to participate. In 2009, Cadets from the Academy still attend the annual Harvard Model Congress.

In December of 1993, the cadets decided they wanted to try Princeton Model Congress in place of the Harvard trip. We drafted a resolution that would curtail ozone depletion. We not only sponsored the resolution in the Princeton congress, but we published it on the back page of *The Bulletin of the Atomic Scientists* as an open letter from our delegation (pictured in their white dress uniforms) to the Clinton administration and the real U. S. Congress. We received a brief acknowledgment from President Clinton and a lengthy reply from Vice President Gore.

The years 1985-2009 have been the happiest years of my life. I spent the first eleven years of this period working at Army Navy Academy with a part-time evening assignment teaching history at Mira Costa College in Oceanside. During this period our family lived in a condo in Quail Ridge in Oceanside, and later in a beautiful mobile home park with attractive greenbelt and nine man-made lakes. Later I worked at Palomar College as an adjunct in history, and for brief periods, part-time, in the Park University Extension Division, teaching American foreign policy, as well as at National University in the teacher preparation and credentialing program.

In 2009, as I approach my 80th birthday, I have a 60% teaching assignment at a Vanguard Institution, Palomar College. A few details of my educational philosophy and strategies (Appendix IX), a list of my major publications (Appendix X), a look at my hobbies (Appendix XI), and a review of my heroes and inspirational figures (Appendix XII) are appended to this work.

In 2002 Ashley Jo Bagnall graduated from El Camino High School (Appendix III).

Ashley Jo Bagnall *Jerry Bryan photo*

Ashley is finishing her senior year at the University of California at San Diego. Naomi still works at her long time job at Wedbush Morgan Securities, and our family lives in Oceanside, in a comfortable home, with our Golden Retriever named Milo and our Chocolate Lab named Samantha.

Chapter Eight:
Career Summary and Life Statement

An abridged curriculum vitae follows:

From 1955-1959, as an elementary school teacher, I taught a simplified survey of American history.

From 1959-1961, I taught the United States history course at Monterey High School and at Monterey Peninsula College.

From 1961-1964, I taught the U.S. History survey at Millikan High School in Long Beach, California.

From 1964-1970, I taught it again at Fullerton College.

From 1970-1982 I served as an administrator at Santa Barbara City College.

From 1982-1985 I taught United States history, as a substitute teacher, in Salt Lake City high schools.

From 1985-1998 I taught survey courses in American History, as an adjunct at MiraCosta College

From 1998 to the present (2009) I have taught United States History at Palomar College. In addition I have a plaque on my wall which was awarded for seven years service, as an adjunct at Park University, teaching American foreign policy.

In the fall of 2009 I will be included in the latest *Who's Who in America*.

Joseph A. Bagnall

The Significance of United States History

In my view, the significance of United States history is that it provides us with an American Testament, a splendid record of human achievement under the oldest written constitution on earth. This record is the story of an enduring federal union,. a union that has survived the transition from an agricultural to an industrial society, a momentous civil war, the monumental economic collapse of the Great Depression, two world wars, and numerous other foreign and domestic challenges. In addition, the American nation emerged from the second world war and a forty year challenge known as the Cold War, as the super power of the world.

But what does this record of American achievement mean in the troubled, tentative, world of 2009? A pantheon of statesmen and scientists have reminded us that in order to survive in the world of environmental and nuclear threats we must build a world security system. John F. Kennedy repeatedly called for a strengthened United Nations and the development of enforceable world law (1:3-82). In his First State of the Union message, President Truman called for the development "of the United Nations organization as the representative of the world as one society" (2) He also organized an international police force, fighting under a U.N. flag to contain North Korean aggression. President Eisenhower called for a world community under law, and in a dramatic letter sent to Senator Hubert Humphrey, called for the strengthening of the International Court of Justice (3:128-130). Albert Einstein, in an address on NBC television on February 19, 1950, called for a world security system (4:302). This plea was repeated numerous times in the book, *Einstein on Peace*, published in 1960. Dr. Edward Teller, Father of the H. Bomb (5:209), and Walter Cronkite, broadcast journalist (6:128), have sounded similar themes.

A compelling case for the United States Constitution as a model for a world security system can be made. I believe I have done so in many books. (Appendix X). In a battered, tentative world, suffering from environmental assaults and facing obliteration with nuclear weapons, it is imperative, in the words of Franklin D. Roosevelt, that we "move forward with strong and active faith."

The Case for American Federalism

I. In the tradition of American federalism, world federalism, could institutionalize freedom, harbor ideological differences, and foster pluralism and diversity throughout the world. In President John F. Kennedy's words, the "world could be made safe for diversity."

II. The United States' system of checks and balances could be utilized to curb tyranny at the world level by specifying and limiting the powers granted to three strengthened branches of the United Nations.

III. The United States' system of division of powers between the national government and the states could be adapted in a world system with a division of power between world authority and national authority.

IV. World federalism could provide the structure for control of nuclear weapons through the strengthening of the United Nations and the development of enforceable world law.

V. The American federal union has protected millions of acres of national parks and forest reserve. World federalism could protect, for all time, the rain forests and the natural habitat that sustains all life on earth.

VI. The American federal government has been the protector of American freedom since its inception. Patriots who fear that the federal government will destroy our freedoms should be reminded that a sacred Bill of Rights is part of our national constitution. Our federal government is the source of our freedoms and has traditionally protected them far better than our states. Under world federalism, with vigorous enforcement of The Universal Declaration of Human Rights, personal freedom and civil liberties could be protected and promoted worldwide.

VII. The American federal government abolished slavery, extended citizenship and the right of the vote to former slaves, and eventually to women and all citizens who are eighteen years of age. A world federal system could extend freedom, extend the suffrage, and otherwise empower world citizens.

VIII. The American federal government provided subsidies and incentives to private companies in order to develop the nation's railroads and assist in various national improvements. Under world federalism, subsidies and incentives could be granted to develop hydroelectric power sites, solar power, hydrogen power, and other alternatives to destructive fossil fuels.

IX. Under American federalism, massive federal spending held the line against complete economic collapse in the Great Depression, and helped win World War II and the Cold War. Under a world security system, the United States could achieve a peace dividend and divert massive spending for a warfare state into the rebuilding of our cities, repairing and extending our federal highways, improving the nation's schools, and subsidizing an industry of alternative fuels. The private sector could receive contracts through competitive bid in much the same way that we have traditionally financed projects for defense.

X. World federalism, fashioned after American federalism, could be the ultimate American triumph.

Notes

1   Joseph A. Bagnall, *President John F. Kennedy's Grand and Global Alliance: World Order for the New Century.* University Press of America, 1992, pp. 3-82.

2   *Public Papers of the Presidents of the United States, Harry S. Truman, Containing the Messages, Speeches and Statements of the President, January 1, to December 31, 1946.* Washington, D. C., U.S. Government Printing Office, 1962.

3   Dwight D. Eisenhower, *US Department of State Bulletin,* January 25, 1960, v. 42. pp. 128-130.

4   Albert Einstein, "Peace in the Atomic Era," *Vital Speeches of the Day*, March 1, 1950. p. 302.

5   Edward Teller, *The Legacy of Hiroshima*, New York: Doubleday and Company, 1962. p. 209.

6   Walter Cronkite, *A Reporter's Life.* Alfred A. Knopf, 1997, p. 128.

Addendums

Addendum #1 in 2012

Early Childhood Landmarks

Salt Lake City 1935

My summer with my family in Salt Lake City was glorious. My pre school class was special. There was a speed boat ride in Liberty Park. For the first time I saw an airplane in flight. These were some of the highlights of my early life.

Kozy Theater Moroni, Utah, 1936-1940

My full time summer job riding the hay horse, 8 hrs a day, 6 days per week, made a trip to the Kozy Theater, five miles away, a special thrill. My grandparents took me at least once a week. Early movies that were significant to me were: Tarzan pictures, Tom Sawyer, Huckleberry Finn, and Shirley Temple and Jane Withers pictures; Walt Disney's first full length animation classic, Snow White and the Seven Dwarfs (1937), was a huge event for me.

Early Childhood Trauma

Schoolyard Brawl 1938

In the Great Depression the school yard at Lincoln School (Moroni, Utah) was bereft of any kind of playground equipment. It was a barren dirt square where girls played skip ("jump") rope, and boys played games of tag and ran races. There were also various kinds of games with marbles..

A popular game with marbles was called "Purg." Two or three boys would dig three holes spaced about 8 yards apart. Then each boy, in turn, would get down on his knees and shoot his marble (with a cocked fist) toward the first hole. If he made a hole in one, he could continue until he missed. The winner, of course was the boy who could shoot his marble in the third hole first.

The name 'Purg" was derived from the fact that the holes were pointed toward purgatory. On a hot dry day our overalls got dusty and smudged. On a wet day they became muddy. In either case they looked like hell.

When we got tired of the same old routines on the playground. we would invent new ways to entertain ourselves. One day a sizable group decided to play "War." So we raided an adjacent corn field where the harvest had been gleaned. The dried up old corn stalks made excellent spears. The battle began when we started throwing corn stalks at one another. My aim was faulty, and I hit a big kid who was not part of our game. He came at me with flailing fists. His ring took a major chip out of my permanent front teeth, and he finished me off with a bloody nose. I ran to the classroom and my teacher sent me home. It was a long tearful walk. No punishment was mentioned for anyone.

Chester Ranch May 10, 1942

It was Mother's Day and my beloved grandfather died from a long bout with internal cancer. I was in the room when he passed. Afterward I gave my grandmother her Mother's Day present.

Childhood Science Lesson

In spite of the lack of equipment at Lincoln Elementary, the teachers were dedicated and they did their best to provide a sound academic experience for us. For example, I recall one day when there was to be an eclipse of the sun. At the appointed time the fourth, fifth and sixth grades were sent to the playground to view the event. The custodian had built a huge bon fire and thrown broken glass on the black, smoldering embers. He then raked the charred glass out, and allowed it to cool. The teachers helped us choose a piece of cool, smoked, thick glass to view the event. Pieces were carefully chosen and we all saw the event without mishap.

Childhood Friends

Joseph and Donnell, 1937

Special childhood friends in the period 1936-1940 were Donnell Blackham and Ray Kelson.

Donnell's father owned the local service station. Donnell had interesting toys. I was fascinated with his 16 mm movie projector which was not really a toy. As a matter of fact it was the standard projector for classroom use until the 1980s.

Donnell studied piano and organ. As an adolescent he played in the Revelers Swing Band, and later he became Student Body President at Moroni High School. As an adult he was a Professor in the field of music at Brigham Young University.

Ray Kelson's father was the industrial arts teacher at Moroni High School. In adult life Ray became a dentist in Riverside, California.

****

Addendum #2 in 2012

Significant Happenings since the First Edition

Joseph A. Bagnall has at least one thing in common with Clint Eastwood, Morgan Freeman, Alan Arkin, Robert Vaughn, Donna Reed,and Esther Williams. We are all listed as Prominent Alumni of Los Angeles City College. The aforementioned are listed in the field of entertainment, and I am listed in the field of education. Google **The LACC Foundation** and go to the Distinguished Alumni link for the complete list.

Appendices

Appendix I: Florence Noland Bagnall

Letter from Mrs. J. Bracken Lee

Letter from President George Albert Smith

Mother of the Year Merit Winner
Arcadia News Post. No Longer Published.

STATE OF UTAH

GOVERNOR'S RESIDENCE
603 EAST SOUTH TEMPLE
SALT LAKE CITY 2, UTAH

J. BRACKEN LEE
GOVERNOR

October 18, 1950

Dear Mrs. Bagnall,

Mrs. Henrod and I wish to express our appreciation for your kindly hospitality, so pleasantly extended us yesterday afternoon in your charming home. We both enjoyed being there so much.

We were impressed by the friendliness and enthusiasm of the nice reception accorded us. We arrived home shortly after 11 PM, feeling we had spent a wonderful day.

Especially, will we remember how lovely your table was in its "royal" color decoration. It was unusual and most attractive against the white curtains, with the afternoon sunshine filtering through. It was cheerful and heart warming.

I hope that I may have the opportunity of seeing you again before too long.

With kindest regards,

Mrs. J. Bracken Lee

177

January 27, 1947

Mr. and Mrs. J. R. Bagnall
North Sanpete Stake
Mt. Pleasant, Utah

Dear Brother and Sister Bagnall:

On my return from Idaho I found a beautiful volume on my desk. The cover is embossed in gold with these words, "These Our Fathers," and the cover is decorated beautifully with an ox team, a covered wagon and a horseman with his gun ready, typical of pioneer days.

I appreciate this beautiful gift very much, and it will repose in my library with more than twenty-five hundred volumes as one of the most beautiful of all. I thank you most sincerely for your gift and assure you I will enjoy perusing it from cover to cover. Every page is intensely interesting to me.

I congratulate the Daughters of the Utah Pioneers of Sanpete County on producing so beautiful a record.

My first knowledge of Sanpete County was about 1884 when I accompanied my father, John Henry Smith, in a comfortable carriage drawn by two horses. Father visited the settlements as far south as Mayfield and in most cases stayed at the homes of the Bishops, where we were treated royally.

The portraits of the various camps of the Daughters of the Pioneers tell a story of real character and I congratulate you on the intelligent, fine appearance of the descendants of the pioneers of Sanpete County. I commend you not only for calling attention to the fathers of the pioneers but also the mothers. I am sure those early pioneers, who long since have passed to their eternal reward, are proud of their descendants and the record they have made.

Again thanking you for your kind remembrance and wishing you and your loved ones every blessing that you can desire, I am

Your brother in the Gospel,

Geo Albert Smith

B.

170

Arcadia News-Post
'Mother of the Year' merit winner

MRS. FLORENCE N. BAGNALL

ARCADIA -- In her front yard is a big, beautiful alder tree. You walk in the house and you get the feeling there's a place for everything. And on the coffee table in the living room there's a big, white Bible.

Right away you know you're not in an ordinary home. This is the home of Mrs. Florence N. Bagnall, 1746 Oakwood Ave., who recently was named one of five merit winners in the statewide "Mother of the Year" contest. Judging was based on letters of recommendation, personal meetings with judges, a list of accomplishments, and home, church and family life.

Her husband, Joseph, was a bishop in the Mormon Church.

As an organist, Mrs. Bagnall has played for more than 100 funerals, 58 memorial services for World War II heroes and countless weddings --- and all without a fee.

188

Appendix II: Joseph R. Bagnall

J.R. Bagnall, Marilyn and Joe
Family Snapshot.

Representative Joseph R. Bagnall
Copyright *Salt Lake Tribune*. Used by permission.

J. R. Bagnall Centenary Article
Copyright *Daily Herald*. All rights reserved. Used by permission.

Joseph A. Bagnall

Rep. Bagnall Talks to World;

J. R. Bagnall ... Sanpete stockman numbers his unseen radio friends with his next door neighbors.

MT. PLEASANT, Sanpete County, Dec. 16 —Since 1934 Rep. J. R. Bagnall (R., Sanpete) has been a "ham."

Not the kind you hang in a smokehouse. Not the kind you see on the stage. Rep. Bagnall is a "ham" radio operator.

From his home in Mt. Pleasant he talks to fellow amateur radio enthusiasts all over the country. His call letters, W7KUC and W7LOH are known by buddies in crowded cities and remote hamlets all over this nation.

'Fun Experimenting'

This voice contact with people he hasn't met is what the personable Sanpete county stock grower likes about his after-sundown pastime. "You get to know a lot of fellows in this hobby," he explains, "and it is fun experimenting."

Come January, brown-haired, medium height Mr. Bagnall is going to meet a lot more fellows. Some, perhaps, he will meet in debate, others in committee sessions and still others on the bus that runs up to capitol hill.

For this is the 48-year-old Mt. Pleasant native's first session in Utah state legislature.

His Friends Insisted

Though an active Republican for a number of years, it was not until friends in the party insisted he run for the house that the former school superintendent entered a contest for political office.

On his ranch "across the county" from Mt. Pleasant, Rep. Bagnall and his cousin, L. R. Bagnall, run several herds of sheep and a number of Hereford steers. Much of the feed this stock consumes is grown on the Bagnall farm.

The representative comes by his ranching naturally. His father started the business, and Rep. Bagnall took over. For six years, though, he combined part-time ranching with a full-time job as superintendent of schools.

Studied Geology at U.

At the University of Utah, which he entered after attending Snow college in nearby Ephraim, the former school teacher studied geology.

And how does geology jibe with stock growing? According to Rep. Bagnall it doesn't jibe at all. "I have never used that geological training," he admits.

Graduating from the university, he also attended Utah State Agricultural college and Brigham Young university, where he earned enough credit for a master's degree, but "didn't complete the formalities."

Serves as Bishop

In his comfortable home four ocks from Mt. Pleasant's business center, Rep. Bagnall lives ith his wife and two well-mannered children. A cocker spaniel lled Sandy completes the household.

An active churchman, Rep. Bagnall has served as bishop of Mt. leasant North ward, Church of Jesus Christ of Latter-day Saints, and at present is a member of the presidency of North Sanpete stake.

Happy to serve Sanpete citizens as one of their two representatives, conscientious J. R. Bagnall is most interested in economy and "efficient government." When he goes up to Salt Lake City this radio "ham" will tune in on both.

Joseph A. Bagnall

THE DAILY HERALD (www.HarkTheHerald.com)   WEDNESDAY, OCTOBER 25, 2000

Centenarian

Educator celebrates 100th birthday, reflects on achievements

By KAREN HOAG
The Daily Herald

PROVO — His place was a gathering spot for youth. Kids felt comfortable in the Bagnall home.

Joseph R. Bagnall, of Provo, turned 100 this week. He and his late wife, Florence, had two children, 11 grandchildren and 17 great grandchildren.

His daughter Marilyn Richards, 68, also of Provo, said, "The neighborhood was always at our house. He'd come home from work in Mt. Pleasant and tell us, 'Go get your bathing suits; let's go swimming and (Reservoir).' "

Joseph spent most of his life in education. He taught elementary school in Salem and Mt. Pleasant and then history and social science at Moroni High School. Next he was superintendent of North Sanpete School District.

The educator served with Gov. J. Bracken Lee in the Utah State legislature; he was elected to two terms. Joseph resigned when Marion D. Romney called him in the early 1950s to be manager of the Church of Jesus Christ of Latter-day Saints' Southern California Regional Welfare Ranch in Perris, Calif.

Next, he served as administrator in an adult education program in Arcadia, Calif., and then as principal of a middle school in the same city.

As a father, LDS bishop and stake president, he made sure Marilyn and her friends always went to their church meetings.

Bagnall met his wife while teaching at Moroni. He was in charge of taking a group of girls to a dance. His mother told him, "Put your suit on and dance with them." He had planned to drop them off and sit back and

> "Just live. Take all the chances you can and land upright."
>
> — Joseph Bagnall

watch. However, he followed his mom's advice and got on the dance floor.

That's when he noticed Florence. "I was going north and she was going south in another dance group," Bagnall said. "She looked sideways at me. I thought to myself, 'She should be the mother of your children.' "

One of his friends introduced them, but when he asked her to dance, she looked at her dance book and found it was full. "She walked away and I walked beside her and asked, 'How about a date Sunday night?' " he said.

After she answered, (he) forgot to find out where she lived. But he did his sleuthing.

Joseph has great memories of Florence and him playing in Lynn's Melodians, an orchestra that was a hit around Sanpete County. He played saxophone and she played piano. Florence liked to write plays, compiling genealogy and history; she edited the centennial history of Sanpete County, "These Our Fathers."

Bagnall's son Joe, 70, of Oceanside, Calif., came home for his dad's 100th year party and said, "One of the special gifts he received for his birthday is a book written by (my mother). It's a long lost book with a special inscription by her."

The book was discovered on the Internet in a rare book shop in Clearwater, Fla., according to Joe.

Joseph and Florence moved back to Utah and the Provo area in 1966. Knowing his love of children, LDS leaders asked Joseph and Florence to teach a Primary class when he was close to 90.

"They taught the children to keep journals," Marilyn said.

"He was always interested in young people, a friend to the fatherless

Achievement: Joseph Bagnall turns 100 on Oct. 23 and is living at Prestige Assisted Living in Provo. He was given a certificate by Gov. Mike Leavitt for reaching his hundredth year.

SAM LUND/The Daily Herald

and those who needed special attention."

She remembers a 7-year-old boy came to their home when her dad was stake president. Joseph went to the door and talked to him.

Afterward, Marilyn asked her dad, "What was that about?"

As it happened, the young boy got into trouble when he stole money

from his bishop, who was a merchant. Joseph counseled with him and said, "Don't steal again; when you need money come to me."

The boy wanted to go to a movie and asked Joseph for cash to buy a ticket. The stake president complied.

Joseph now lives in Prestige Assisted Living Center.

This meat and potatoes man who is a centenarian, father, grandfather, church leader, educator and legislator has advice to those wanting to attain his longevity:

"Just live. Take all the chances you can and land upright."

Karen Hoag can be reached at 344 2542 or khoag@heraldextra.com.

Appendix III:
Friends in the Formative Years

Joe and Richard in Surrey

Richard B. Hansen

Richard Hansen was the son of the Mayor of Mt. Pleasant, Utah. His father lost most of his local real estate properties in the Great Depression. He also passed away when Richard was very young. My father hired Richard to work on our ranch, so Richard and I worked together each summer throughout our adolescent years. When he became old enough to have a driver license, we "double dated."

As a young man Richard was bold and adventuresome. He played fullback on the North Sanpete High football team, he dived from high rocks into the lake at Palisade Park, and he climbed the water tower at the railroad station in Spring City and plunged into the water for a risky night time swim. Immediately after high school he joined the naval reserve and went to sea for two weeks in the summer.

As an adult he served in the Korean War and remained in the National Guard thereafter. He rose in the ranks in the Guard to ultimately become a full Colonel, commanding Special Forces in four states. In the interim he had served with distinction as a paratrooper and worked in the advertising department at the *Deseret News* in Salt Lake City.

Childhood and Adolescence

As a child my basketball buddies were my closest friends. Don McIntosh, Arthur O. Neilson, Jr., Wally Beck, Victor Jensen, and Ted Kay.

Arthur became a football coach at Richfield High School and a biology teacher in Utah Schools. Don became a basketball coach at American Fork High School, contending for the Utah state championship by placing in the top five teams on four occasions, and winning it once. He later coached basketball at University of Southern Colorado. Wally Beck was a basketball star who played briefly at BYU and in the service. When he returned from his stint in the army, he transferred to the University of Utah, pledged to Sigma Chi fraternity and pursued a pre-dental major. He became a dentist. Victor Jensen and I "double dated" and got caught up in rivalries over girl friends. Victor served in the field of education in various administrative positions, as a teacher, and as a mayor of a small town. Ted Kay was a close friend who later owned an automobile business and was a private pilot. Arthur Lee Monson became Salt Lake County Treasurer. NACTFO gave him the Outstanding Treasurer in America Award in 1988.

Other friends at North Sanpete High School include John K. Madsen Olsen. He served a Mormon Mission in France, returned to finish his degree at the University of Utah and then went on to Stanford Law School. Since that time he has served as the President of The Canada Montreal Mission of the Church of Jesus Christ of Latter-day Saints, become a successful investor and developed an impressive law practice. Louis Peterson became a successful MD with a specialty in ophthalmology. Charles McKay remained in Mt. Pleasant and operated a successful business there. His daughter returned to Mt. Pleasant to set up her office as a Physician's Assistant, while her husband served the area as an accountant.

There were many more success stories connected with North Sanpete High School. These are just a few that fell into my age range and my circle of friends. To our upstate urban sophisticates we were all lumped together as Sanpete "carrot eaters" ---country cousins from the back country. But how could they have known then that we were descendants of Mormon pioneers and the children of *The Greatest Generation*, destined to do important things with our lives. I am proud of my classmates and the place that at one time we all called home.

Appendix IV:
South High Choir Invitation

South High Scribe

South Hi Choir Will Perform in Pasadena

THE SOUTH HIGH SCHOOL a capella choir, under the direction of Armont Willardsen, will sing at the Music Educators National Conference, California-Western Division, at Pasadena, Calif., April 13, it was announced Saturday.

Authorization for the appearance was given by the Salt Lake City Board of Education after consideration of an invitation presented through Amy Grau Miller, president of California-Western division.

In addition to singing at the general session of the biennial meeting of the conference, the choir will also demonstrate contemporary music at a clinical session, according to Mr. Willardsen. It also plans to tour the San Francisco Bay area before returning to Salt Lake City.

Under Mr. Willardsen, the choir has gained wide prominence for its a cappella work. The conductor is a graduate of the University of Utah and Northwestern University, where he took his master's degree in music. He is national president of Kappa Gamma Psi, national music fraternity.

Recently the choir was heard on the Payson Community Concert series and will be heard in four programs in Salt Lake City during the next two weeks. Dates will be announced later.

DIRECTOR — Armont Willardsen, will take South High Choir to Pasadena, Calif., for Music Educators' meet.

Appendix V: Deseret News Roundtable

Copyright *Deseret News,* Used by permission.

Joseph A. Bagnall

S. L. Students Favor Rationing

Weekly High School Forum Discusses President's Suggestion
Concludes That Consumption, Price Controls Are Needed

This week's Forum question "Should the president re-establish rationing?" roused such a lively discussion that it was very evident that local high school students are really thinking—and thinking hard—about national issues.

Taking part in the discussion were Richard Winters, 16, 380 E Street, Senior at East High; Hank Moyle, 17, 5450 Highland Drive, Granite High Senior; Dale Mitchell, 18, 755 Blair, and a Senior at West, and Joe Bagnall, 17, 555 East First South, a South Senior.

RICHARD sparked the discussion by saying that he believed everyone was agreed that we had to do something to help Europe and that the rationing program would be set up for that purpose mainly.

"But I think we will need something other than just a rationing program," he went on. "I have read that in six up such a program and get it into operation it would take three this time is essential. In that three months, Europe will starve.

"Therefore, we can't go into operation immediately with any kind of plan that will get help to Europe right away.

"President Truman has asked Congress to give him the power to put to work whatever plan he thinks best, and this raises the question of whether Congress should give such authority—which is almost dictatorial to the president, particularly in times of peace.

Democracy Slow But Careful

"A democracy is slow in action but when it acts it expresses the will of the people, and it seems to me that if Congress grants the president this power, it will actually be what the people want—as expressed by their representatives.

"I think that rationing should be set up right away, even if it takes some time—particularly if it is going to take some time not only in order to help Europe, but also to curb prices and to prevent any further inflation than we have now, as well as to safeguard us from a terrible depression.

"I think that the people are trying to realize what the conditions in Europe actually are—that they want to help—and that whatever steps are taken will be taken carefully and intelligently."

DALE was decidedly for a rationing program.

Rationing Has Worked

"Under rationing, everyone would be equally able to purchase the necessities of life, while with the rising costs of these basic items only the fortunate can buy them. I work in a grocery store and from what I see, I am convinced that under as a rule have a lower standard of living than they had during the war. That is, I mean that the average family actually has less of the basic food and clothing than they had under rationing.

"During the war rationing was ordered to equalize the distribution of food and clothing while we were shipping large quantities of goods to our soldiers and allies. Well now we still have to ship basic goods to Europe, and the same method of equalizing should be adopted to relieve stress here at home. It worked during the war and it will work again.

Dale Mitchell

"I realize that such a plan means relinquishing some individual rights, but in times of emergency, the American people have always been willing to give up some individual rights for the common good. I think that now, after we have seen what has happened with price controls removed, everyone will be more willing to support rationing honestly, and this would do a lot toward eliminating the bad aspects of the system—the black market, and so on."

"Some people claim that the Republicans are against a system of rationing because the Democrats suggested it—and the Republicans think it is a good vote-getting scheme, but I think the problem should be outside of politics and should be dependent upon the actual needs and the best interests of all the people.

"I believe rationing will have to be routed but only for those necessities made scarce by our help to Europe. That would leave a broad field of goods from which the average family could supplement its rationed supplies and still maintain a high level of living.

"These basic items would include standard foods, clothing, housing, and fuel.

"We could then send these goods to Europe, priming their production machine until it gets going full speed. Then, when the world's economy is more balanced, we can remove the controls again.

"Personally, I think we here in the United States have too many luxuries, anyway. History has shown that when a country or a race becomes accustomed to luxury, it soon deteriorates and falls. We haven't

R. Winters

Hank Moyle

Joe Bagnall

should be imposed on us, if we wish to survive.

"In that way, I agree with Richard that rationing is for our own good as much as for Europe's.

JOE agreed.

"The president asked the people to take voluntary action—to curtail buying voluntarily—in order to have supplies to send to Europe. But it didn't do much good. People went right on buying just what they wanted—whether they needed it or not—providing they could pay for it.

"Voluntary rationing hasn't worked. But we must have some sort of control over consumption and prices if we are going to get anywhere at all, either here or abroad. Here, we can see that prices keep climbing and wages climbing right after prices, trying to catch up—but never quite doing it. And we're headed for a depression just as sure as this keeps on.

"Well then, about all that can be done is to impose rationing on the people until production catches up with demand, and that will probably be some time because we are sending so much of our manufactured goods and food away.

"There is one big problem, of course—Will we have to go through all this again when price controls are finally removed? But whether we do or not, the only thing to do right now, it seems to me, is to put on a good, strong rationing program and support it wholeheartedly. We made mistakes before, but even so we're better off than if we had had no pro-

68

Appendix VI: The Vern Gardner Story

The Daily Utah Chronicle. University of Utah student newspaper.

Vern Gardner's No. 33 will be retired in the Utah sports hall of fame tomorrow at the annual song fest. Only Ferrin's No. 22 has received this distinction. Arnie's was honored last year.

Gardner's No. 33 Retired Tomorrow

By JOE BAGNALL

Another bright page of athletic history will be written into the annals of Utah's sports glory when Vern Gardner's famous 33 will be retired as a special feature on Thursday night's stadium songfest.

Thus Gardner joins the immortal Ute, Arnie Ferrin, whose number was retired in a game against Wyoming at the field house last year. These Ute casaba greats have warmed nets all over the nation to lead Utah's colors to the basketball hall of fame.

Tribute has been paid big Vern this season as a nation of spectators heralded his play, and jested the renaming of Madison Square Garden after the popular Ute.

Aspiring to all-American selection for the third consecutive year, and to all-conference honors for the fourth, the big fellow has won distinction as a prominent sports figure.

His first prestige came in 1947 when he was named the NIT's most valuable player. Here he led Utah to the national championship.

Since the big Ute's first campaign as a frosh, his success has grown to climax in his representing the west as one of a galaxy of collegiate all-stars in Madison Square Garden play in March. And as this Utah great concludes his college career, he focuses attention on the offers from professional leagues. He reserves decision as yet, and possibly will continue to do so until contract deadline.

In the Basketball Association of America league, Vern has been drafted by the Phillies, and is thus ineligible for another team in the same pro-loop.

Appendix VII: Junior Prom Article, Herald Express Clippings

Copyright *Deseret News*. Used by permission
Los Angeles Herald Express. No longer publishing.

Joseph A. Bagnall

The Deseret News

Salt Lake City, Utah, Thursday Evening, February 6, 1947

PREPARE FOR PROM—Officers of North Sanpete High School who will direct the annual prom. Sitting, left to right, Carolyn Madsen, junior class vice president; Kennith Osborn, class president; Maurine Schofield, class secretary-treasurer. Standing, Joseph Bagnall, prom master, Afton Anderson, reporter; Norma Jensen, prom mistress. The prom and post-prom will be held this weekend.

North Sanpete High Awaits Annual Prom

MT. PLEASANT — In a fairyland of vari-colored beams from the sun, which is bringing "Daybreak" once more to the world, the Juniors of North Sanpete High School will be feted at their annual Junior Prom and post-prom, Friday and Saturday, Feb. 7 and 8, at the Armory Hall.

The theme of "Daybreak" offers a myriad of ideas in the decorative line, and the effect which the Juniors have managed to produce are beautiful and unique. Centered on one wall is a huge oil painting of the theme by one of Utah's prominent artists, Mr. Max Blain. Towers of many colors, an attractive "Juniors '48" sign, and special accents around the orchestra platform, add color and interest to the central theme of the lovely decorations. Special lighting gives a desirable effect.

Committees Named

Committees for the day and evening are: assembly, LaMar Hamilton, chairman; Phyllis McArthur, co-chairman; advertisement, Mary Anderson; lighting, Robert Olsen; dance programs, Mary Louise Madsen; show case decorations, Helen Rasmussen; prom decorations, Parry Sorensen, chairman, Carolyn Peel, co-chairman; faculty advisors, V. H. Gunderson, Max Blain, Darlene Bell, Gordon Brunger; officers, Joe Bagnall, prom master; Norma Jensen, prom mistress; Kenneth Osborne, president; Carolyn Madsen, vice president; Maurine Schofield, secretary-treasurer; Afton Anderson, reporter.

The Book Parade

Pentagon Politics

(Reviewed by Joseph A. Bagnall)

Why does the Pentagon continue to purchase obsolete weapons in the age of atomic warfare? Why were atomic bomb secrets released for public information shortly after Hiroshima? These questions are answered in "PENTAGON POLITICS"—a new book written by Col. William H. Neblett, past national president of the Reserve Officers Association, and published by the Pageant Press.

According to Colonel Neblett our fighting men are being equipped with obsolete weapons because Pentagon staff officers put their own self advancement before the task of obtaining better defense weapons. He also blames a glory seeking officer for revealing much information about the atomic bomb.

Startling revelations of big brass politics fill the pages of the colorful new book, as Colonel Neblett criticizes many who are held in high regard. Always he mentions names and refers to specific events.

Colonel Neblett further explains that our defense system is outmoded. In his opinion it is rigged to call for a huge conscript army partly to retain some of the top brass in power. He believes that we should replace our huge standing army with a democratic organization similar to the Swiss style of citizen soldiery. Colonel Neblett says this type of defense organization would facilitate our security measures by placing an emphasis on modern military planning and equipment.

HERALD EXPRESS

DAVID W. HEARST, PUBLISHER

SATURDAY, FEBRUARY 28, 1953

The Book Parade
What Los Angeles Is Reading

Make the U. N. Effective for Peace
(Reviewed by Joseph A. Bagnall)

Dr. John Bauer cites the primary requisite of world peace in his new book "MAKE THE U. N. EFFECTIVE FOR PEACE," published by Richard R. Smith, is the formation of an effective world police force.

To accomplish peace seems futile as suspicious world powers continue a rapid armament race. Armament races such as these have never either promoted or preserved peace, and thus Dr. Bauer recommends a revised United Nations charter to facilitate world tranquillity.

World peace hopes have been frustrated in the present United Nations due to the distrust that prevails between members. The United States should propose that the United Nations be reconstituted to provide intrinsic power to make and enforce laws to bring about security.

The aims of the new agency should be:

1. Prohibit aggression.
2. Prohibit National Armaments.
3. Enforce the dual prohibitions.

Dr. Bauer believes that an international police force is the answer to world peace and he points out that the reorganized United Nations would succeed only through the consent and participation of the nations.

Dr. Bauer believes that peace in world can be accomplished and that Communism can be halted.

Romans, Hollywood In Finals

Los Angeles High thumped a Banning High cage entry 38 to 32 and Hollywood High breezed past Marshall 58 to 42 in yesterday's semifinal round of the city high school basket playoffs.

Thus it will be Romans vs. Hollywood High when Friday rolls around and it comes time to decide the city high school basketball champions.

Yesterday's clash between Hollywood and Marshall at LACC was completely dominated by a well balanced Hollywood quint that used a fast-breaking screen and hand off attack.

It was this bit of strategy that enabled the Hollywood lads to break into the hapless Marshall defense and score repeatedly at close range. The point happy Hollywood five were able to use substitutions freely during the final period, and so they capitalized on their reserve strength to win in a walk. Big Jim Kokum carried the brunt of Hollywood's well distributed scoring attack, as he garnered 19 points to lead all individual scoring for the tussle.

Marshall's Hubbard and B. Walker provided scoring punch for the losers, with nine points each, but they bowed to Teammate Laemmle who got 13 for the honors.

LOS ANGELES	G.	Ft.	Pf.	T.	BANNING	G.	Ft.	Pf.	T.
Kaufmn,f	5	7	2	17	Schuler,f	3	3	2	9
Tusan,f	3	3	4	9	Quebec,f	0	1	5	1
Strubing,c	0	0	2	0	Richrds,c	6	6	0	18
White,g	3	1	2	7	Raine,g	1	2	2	4
Shapiro,g	0	3	2	3	Watkns,g	0	0	2	0
Hargrves,c	0	0	2	0	Mlidvch,f	0	0	0	0
Morton,g	1	0	1	2					
Cooke,c	0	0	0	0					
Totals	12	14	15	38	Totals	10	12	11	32

SCORE BY QUARTERS

Los Angeles	3	6	14	15—38
Banning	6	6	11	9—32

Free throws missed: Los Angeles—Kaufman 3; Morton, Shapiro. Banning—Richards, 4; Raine, 3; Schuler, 2; Milidenovich, 2; Quebec.

Officials—Ken Fagans and Bill Russell.

HOLLYWOOD	G.	Ft.	Pf.	T.	MARSHALL	G.	Ft.	Pf.	T.
Friedmn,f	3	2	1	8	K.Wlkr,f	0	2	4	2
Cuthbert,f	5	0	2	10	Kinder,f	2	1	1	5
Yocum,c	8	3	0	19	Laemle,c	2	9	2	13
Rosenbrg,g	3	2	3	8	B.Wlkr,g	4	1	2	9
Pope,g	3	1	4	7	Sawyer,g	0	0	0	0
Matteson,f	0	0	1	0	Blkman,f	1	2	2	4
Hix,f	0	0	1	0	Hubbrd,g	3	3	3	9
Breger,g	0	4	2	4					
Thomas,g	0	2	1	2					
Totals	22	14	15	58	Totals	12	18	14	42

SCORE BY QUARTERS

Hollywood	13	11	19	15—58
Marshall	3	11	11	20—42

Free throws missed: Hollywood—Cuthbert, Yocum 2, Pope, Rosenberg, Breger. Marshall—K. Walker 2, Laemmle, Kinder.

Officials—Bud Brubaker and John Selwood.

Appendix VIII: International Day Story

The Hornet Fullerton Junior College student newspaper.

Joseph A. Bagnall

Radio-Phone Debate Highlights International Day Festival

A three - hour radio - telesymposium on United States policy in Vietnam and China featuring cross-country communication with Senators Robert F. Kennedy, John Tower and others, will highlight the first annual Fullerton Junior College International Day April 21.

PANEL DISCUSSION

The radio-telesymposium will be conducted in the Campus Theatre on North Lemon Street with a part of FJC International Club students posing questions to the Senators in Washington D.C. Communication will be carried by radio and telephone. Joel A. Spivak of radio station KLAC will moderate the panel.

Students and faculty members of the college are also hopeful that Mark Hatfield, Senator from Ore-

start with registration and refreshments from 9 to 10 a.m. and a Karate exhibition in the men's gymnasium from 10 to 11 a.m. From 11 to 12:15, there will be a showing of the award winning color movie "Albert Schweitzer" in the Student Center.

From 12-2 p.m. lunch may be purchased. Spanish and Hawaiian dancing will be featured on the lawn. Dr. Hershey has expressed interest in "Saturday on the Grass" with such topics as the foreign student in Orange County, Chinese shadow boxing, Chinese music, folk singing, ethnic humor, etc. Signs will be posted. The radio-telesymposium will start at 3 p.m. in the Campus Theatre.

EVENING EVENTS

From 5:15 to 6:30, guests will watch a soccer game between the

ROBERT KENNEDY
. . . Debates Saturday

gon, may be able to participate. The day-long activities will

FJC International Club and Chaffey Colleges on the east field. From 6:30 to 8:30 p.m. foreign students from nine southern California junior colleges will be guests of families in the north Orange County area.

From 8:30 in the evening to midnight, those attending the International Day program may dance to the Disneyland Hotel Band in the Student Center and patio. Registration for the day's events, which are open to the public, is being taken in advance because of limited seating. The registration charge of $3.75 per person may be paid during this week at the student center.

In charge of the event, which will draw students from colleges throughout the area, are Akinola James (Nigeria), Rod Raghaven

JOEL SPIVAK
. . . Program Moderator

JOHN TOWER
. . . Speaking Senator

(India), Charles Liddell (USA) and Joseph A. Bagnall, FJC instructor and club advisor.

THE HORNET
The Official Publication of Fullerton Junior College

Fullerton, California, Friday, April 21, 1967

Vol. XLV   No. 2

FLYING TEACHER
SEE PAGE 3

MALE TAILORS
SEE PAGE 3

80

Appendix IX:
Statement of Philosophy and Practice

Statement of Philosophy and Practice

By Joseph A. Bagnall

Teaching Methodologies

I utilize Performance Based Curriculum with a strong emphasis on mastery of detailed time lines. Students are expected to know the chronology of events and be able to match them with cue phrases that indicate knowledge of the content of the event. I also present topical abstracts that compare and contrast philosophies and focus on conceptual facets of our history. Time lines and sentence fragments are administered in testing in the objective realm, while assigned essays written in ink, in a standard college Blue Book, help me to assess the quality of student responses.

Creating Intimacy

Fullerton College 1968: When I was assigned a class of about 80 students in a terraced choral room setting, I took my Super 8mm movie camera and made a 3 minute pan of the students' faces, row by row. I simultaneously passed around a seating chart for the students to fill in. Next, I took the movie film to an overnight developer and spent 45 minutes associating the names on the seating chart with the faces on my film. As a result I could greet the students by name in my second class session.

Palomar College 1998-2009: In the first class session I always pass out Student Data sheets that help me work effectively with students as individuals. In some large classes I have passed out an office visit schedule form, giving every student an opportunity to schedule a 30 minute visit (in the library or elsewhere) before or after class.

Meeting Individual Needs

Mira Costa College 1988-2000 As an Adjunct at Mira Costa College I had about four Japanese students in my history class. I spent extra hours with them, helping them to deal with the dual task of mastering a new language and a new subject. Very soon my classes had 10 to 15 Japanese students each. When I began teaching at Palomar about 10 to 15 Japanese students began to drive over from Mira Costa to attend my class at Palomar. On average that many still do (for each class).

I encouraged a student to apply for officer training and wrote him a recommendation which was reflective of his academic talent and leadership qualities. He was soon commissioned. There are many examples of success stories in which I have been directly involved. I received a recent e-mail from an attorney in Newport Beach. He was effusive in his thanks for help and guidance in the 1960s. Another e-mail was from a Palomar student who received an A from me. He said that the A was his first since early high school days. He said that he was currently receiving good grades.

Empowering Students--The College Supplementary Reader

Mira Costa College 1994 I published a college supplementary reader titled *The Modern United States History Abstract: A Mini Multi-Cultural Text*. The first part of this text was used by students in an assigned open-book review test---an eleven page "refresher test" always given as a prep for the final examination. The second part of this text contained brief commentary on historical contributions of African-Americans, Mexican-Americans, Native Americans and Women. The bibliography for these minorities approximated 350 items. In a discussion period on African - Americans, for example, each student would be asked to read two articles. With that approach every student was empowered with specific information. The resultant discussion was always stimulating and informative with widespread participation. Research papers and panel reports were also organized utilizing the periodicals listed in the bibliographies. *The Modern United States History Abstract* was re-released later by McGraw Hill and a more current edition has been utilized in my classes until last semester at Palomar College.

Creating Unique Learning Environments

Radio Telesymposium Fullerton College April 22, 1967 As foreign student adviser at Fullerton College, I organized the first annual foreign student day with invited foreign students from nine other campuses in Southern California. Part of the activities was a 3 hour phone debate between Senator Robert F. Kennedy and Senators Tower and Kuchel. Each Senator participated by telephone from his office. At Fullerton College we had Radio KLAC broadcasting the event with our student panel on stage, students lined up at microphones in the auditorium aisles, and callers from the radio audience throughout Southern California all hooked up as questioners of the Senators. (See Appendix IX)

At Palomar College I have involved my history classes in two electronic field trips. The first involved my entire History 102 class in a tele-conference hookup with Dr. Mario Molina at MIT. Our history students could see Dr. Molina and he could see our class. He was questioned for over an hour on his work as co-discoverer of ozone depletion and his resultant Nobel Prize. A reporter from the *San Diego Union* was in attendance and she wrote a nice article covering the event.

The second electronic field trip involved a telephone hookup with Lincoln Scholar Rodney Davis at Knox College in Galesburg, Illinois. Dr. Davis and Dr. Douglas Wilson have made the most significant contribution to' an understanding of Abraham Lincoln in my lifetime. This is how it happened. First, Billy Herndon, Lincoln's law partner, spent the last thirty-five years of his life collecting a massive amount of material on Lincoln's early life. This unorganized material was deposited in the Library of Congress. Davis and Wilson of Knox College spent their lives organizing these documents and indexing them. They can now be purchased in a multi-volume set titled *Herndon's Informants.* It was our privilege as a History 101 class to interview Dr. Davis for one hour on Lincoln's early life. Every class member asked Dr. Davis a question. The interview was edited and shaped into a radio program that was transmitted on a satellite in a soft feed to over 325 National Public Radio stations.

Recently I took my History 102 class to a breakfast meeting of WW II pilots at Denny's Restaurant in Oceanside. WW II pilots have been meeting every Wednesday. morning at this same location for the past twenty years. This event was covered in our Palomar newspaper, *The Telescope.* There was a follow-up mention of our trip with a special commendation in the editorial column of the *North County Times.* This led to my request to Pat Hahn, Director of Radio and Television at Palomar, to record a program involving pilots who were special heroes in terms of missions accomplished and experiences as POW's, etc. As a result a program was taped at KOCT, involving the Palomar student television team. The program, titled "Heroes of the Greatest Generation," aired on KOCT and Palomar TV.

I have a vast assortment of historical documentaries on VHS and DVD. Among them are the only filmed speech of Calvin Coolidge in existence (special order from archives of Library of Congress) and many PBS and History Channel films. My students see these if they come to class 1 hour early. They get 1 point extra credit for each VHS or DVD.

Appendix X: Major Publications

John F. Kennedy's Lost Pathway to Peace

Written and produced by Joseph A. Bagnall

This historic documentary aired on TBS and KCET, the Los Angeles PBS affiliate, on May 29, 1987, the 70th anniversary of JFK's birth. Robert Vaughn narrated this testament to the vision and courage of a president who made heroic proposals to control nuclear weapons and curb environmental deterioration. *DVD*

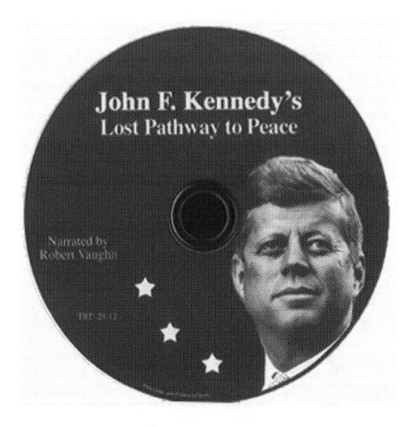

John F. Kennedy: Spokesman for the New Century

Written and Produced by Joseph A. Bagnall

This documentary is a revision and update of the television special titled, "John F. Kennedy's Lost Pathway to Peace." It contains more information on JFK's proposal for a worldwide program of conservation.

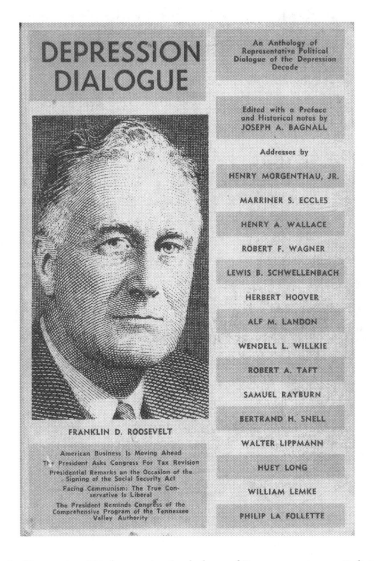

Bagnall, Joseph A. *Depression Dialogue: An Anthology of Representative   Political Dialogue of the Depression Decade.* William C. Brown, 1965.

This book is out of print, but it can be found in the following libraries:

University of California at Irvine
California State University at Long Beach
Los Angeles Public Library
California State University at Northridge
Pima County Community College
University of Arizona
Stanford University Libraries
California State University, Sacramento
California State Library, Sacramento
University of California, Davis
University of Colorado, Boulder
Regis University
Colorado State University
Willammette University
Washington State University
Washington State Library
University of Washington Libraries
Washington University, St Louis
Bradley University
Southern Illinois University
Simon Fraser University
Southern Methodist University
Witchita State University
Emporia State University Texas A and M University
University of Northern Iowa
Clarke College
Louisiana State University
St. Louis Public Library
University of Iowa Library
University of Wisconsin, Madison
University of Illinois
Wisconsin Historical Society
Alabama State University
Indiana University
Northwestern University
University of W. Florida

Atlanta University Center
Auburn University
Bowling Green State University
Kent State University
University of Western Ontario
Winthrop University
Zanesville campus Library
Buffalo and Erie County Public Library
Chatham University
North Carolina State University
SUNY at Buffalo
University of Pittsburg
York University Library, Canada
College of William and Mary
Cornell University
Howard University
Ithaca College Library
Johns Hopkins University
State Library of Pennsylvania
SUNY at Brockport
University of Rochester,
East Stroudsburg University Library
Rutgers University
SUNY at Courtland
Baruch College
Brooklyn College
Columbia University Libraries
Fordham University
New York Public Library
Pace University
SUNY College at Pittsburg
Yale University Library
Brandeis University Library
Brown University

While none of my publications have been popular, they may be found in prestigious places: For example, my first book on President John F. Kennedy was found in the personal library of Linus Pauling, the recipient of two Nobel Prizes, one in chemistry and one in peace. It resides in the Oregon State University special collections where it is included among Pauling's personal books. The entry reads:

JX1974.7.B33 *President John F. Kennedy, A Grand and Global Alliance: the Summons to World Peace through World Law.* Edited by Joseph A. Bagnall, 1968.

This same book can also be found in the following libraries:

California Polytechnic State University, San Luis Obispo
California State University, Fullerton
California State University, Long Beach
California State University, Los Angeles
California State University, Northridge
California State University, Sacramento
Claremont College, CA
Monterey Institute of International Studies, CA
Pepperdine University Law Library, CA
San Diego State University, CA
UCLA, CA
UC Berkeley, CA
UC San Diego, CA
UC Santa Barbara, CA
University of Alaska
Auburn University, AL
Spring Hill College, AL
Arizona State University
University of Arizona
Auroria Library, CO
University of Colorado, Boulder
Yale University
National Defense University Library, Washington, DC
Lake City Community College, FLA
Georgia State University
South Georgia College
University of Georgia, Law School Library
University of MarilynHawaii, Manoa
Northwestern College, IA
University of Iowa
University of Northern Iowa
Loyola University, Chicago Law Library
Northern Illinois University
Northwestern University School of Law
Northwestern University, IL
Southern Illinois University
University of Chicago
University of Illinois, Urbana
Emporia State University, KS
Witchita Public Library, KS
Witchita State University, KS
Boston University, MA

University of Massachusetts, Amherst
University of Maine, School of Law
Eastern Michigan University
Wayne State University, MI
Western Michigan University
Concordia College, MN
University of Minnesota Law Library
Saint Louis Public Library
University of Missouri, KC
Washington University, MO
University of Montana
State Library of North Carolina
University of Nebraska, Kearney
Case Western Reserve University, OH
Case Western Reserve University Law Library, OH
Cleveland State University, OH
Kent State University, OH
Miami University, OH
Ohio State University, College of Law
Ohio State University
Public Library of Cincinnati
Oklahoma State University
Oregon State University
East Stroudsburg University, PA
US Army War College, PA
University of Pennsylvania
University of Pittsburgh
Furman University, SC
Middle Tennessee State University
University of Tennessee
Texas A and M, Corpus Christi
Texas A and M, College Station
Texas State University
University of Utah Law Library
University of Utah
Virginia Tech Coll Analysis
Washington State University
Western Washington University
Ripon College, WI
University of Wisconsin
University of Alberta, Edmonton, Canada
Simon Fraser University, Burnaby, BC
and others.

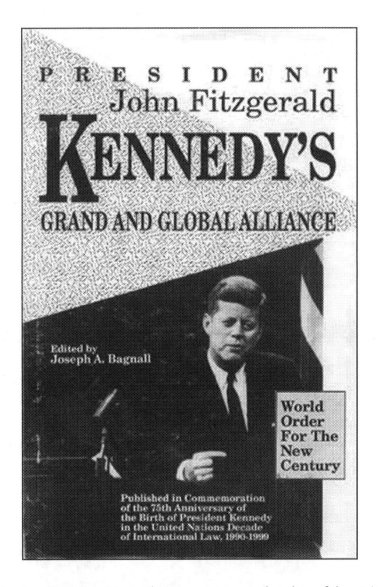

My second book on President Kennedy was a revision and update of the 1968 version. Titled *President John F. Kennedy's Grand and Global Alliance: World Order for the New Century*, it was published by University Press of America in 1992.

Back Cover Endorsements

"An excellent and valuable collection of the Kennedy Legacy--the Kennedy to be remembered and studied."
--Dr. J.W. Peltason
Professor of Political Science, University of California, Irvine
Author of Understanding the Constitution, 12th edition, 1991
Co-author of Government by the People, 14th edition, 1990
Chancellor of the University of California System

"This book reminds one of what a leader can do in the Presidency--John Kennedy's vision makes a sharp contrast to the last ten years of myopia in the White House"
--Dr. Paul R. Ehrlich
Bing Professor of Population Studies, Department of
Biological Sciences, Standford University
Author of The Population Bomb, 1968 and
Extinction: The Causes and Consequences of
the Disappearance of Species, 1981

"Dr. Joseph A. Bagnall's book will give students a new look at Kennedy's proposed global alliance. This is a workable scheme, in Kennedy's own words, of how to develop the international machinery to guarantee freedom, keep the peace, and save the planet from world-wide pollution. The book presents that part of the Kennedy global legacy that has been lost in a welter of Kennedy books that sensationalize rather than instruct."
--Rev. Theodore M. Hesburgh, C.S.C.
President Emeritus of University of Notre Dame

"We will need global agreements to resolve environmental issues such as ozone depletion, and Dr. Bagnall's book documents the fact that President Kennedy set the precedents for such agreements."
--Dr. Mario Molina
Professor of Chemistry & Professor of Earth,
Atmospheric, & Planetary Science
Massachusetts Institute of Technology
Co-Discoverer of Ozone Depletion
Recipient of the Nobel Prize in Chemistry

"A vivid reminder of the hope, energy and vision of the Kennedy years."
--Dr. David M. Kennedy
Department of History, Stanford University
Author of the *American Pageant*, 9th edition, 1991

My second Kennedy book can be found in the following libraries:

Beverly Hills Public Library, CA	University of Georgia
California State University, Chico	West Georgia Tech College
California State University, Fresno	Brigham Young University, Idaho
California State University, Monterey Bay	Columbia College, IL
Los Angeles Public Library	Loyola University of Chicago
Mount St Mary's College	Principia College, Il
Pepperdine University	Indiana University
San Francisco Public Library	University of Notre Dame
University of California, Berkeley	University of Kansas
University of California, Davis	Wichita State University
University of California, Irvine	University of Kentucky
University of California, Merced	Tulane University
University of California, Riverside	Boston College
University of California, San Diego	Emanuel College, MA
University of San Diego	Fitchburg State College, MA
University of the Pacific	Harvard University
UAA/APU, Alaska	Massachusetts Institute of Technology
Auburn University, AL	Northeastern University, Burlington
Jacksonville State University, AL	Northeastern University, Boston
Shelton State Community College, AL	State Library of Massachusetts
Arizona State University	University of Massachusetts at Boston
University of Arizona	US Naval Academy, MD
Auraria Library, CO	Villa Julie College, MD
Colorado State University	Bates College Library, ME
University of Colorado, Boulder	Michigan State University
University of Colorado, Colorado Springs	University of Michigan
Yale University	Missouri State University
American University	University of Missouri, Columbia
Georgetown University	Duke University
National Defense University Library	North Carolina AT and T
University of Delaware	University of North Carolina
Florida International University	University of Nebraska at Lincoln
University of Florida	Princeton University
University of North Florida	University of Nevada, Las Vegas
Atlanta Metropolitan College, GA	Columbia University, NY
Georgia Institute of Technology	Farmingdale State, NY
Georgia State University	Houghton College Library, NY

New York Public Library
US Military Academy, West Point
Ohio State University
Ohio University
Public Library of Cincinnati
University of Akron
University of Toledo
Indiana University of Pennsylvania
Temple University
US Army War College, PA
University of South Carolina
Stephen F. Austin State, TX
Texas A and M
University of Houston
University of Texas, Dallas
University of Texas, El Paso
Brigham Young University
University of Utah
Utah State University
College of William and Mary
Ferum College, VA
George Mason University
Hampden-Sydney College, VA
Old Dominion University, VA
University of Mary Washington
Virginia Historical Society
Marquette University
University of Western Ontario, London
York University Libraries, Toronto
University of Regina, Canada
Staats and und Universitaatsbibliothek, Gottingen, Germany
Hong Kong University of Science and Tech
Waseda University, Tokyo, Japan
British Library, Boston Spa, Wetherby, W Yorkshire, UK
Cambridge University, UK
and others.

The Kennedy Option:

Pursuit of World Law

Joseph Albert Bagnall

My third book on President Kennedy was titled *The Kennedy Option: Pursuit of World Law*. Published by University Press of America, it can be found in many libraries across America.

Arizona State University
Atlanta University Center
Bates College Library
Bethany College
California State University, Fresno
Carsbad (CA) City Library
Central Michigan University
Chapman University School of Law
Cleveland Marshall College of Law
College of William and Mary Law Library
Colorado State University
Columbia University Libraries
Davidson College Library
Duke University Law Library
Eastern Washington University
Fairleigh Dickinson University
Fayetteville University
Fordham University
Franklin and Marshall College
George Mason University
Georgetown University
Georgetown University Law Library
Georgia Institute of Tech
Harvard University, Harvard College Library
Indiana University, South Bend
Indiana University Bloomington
Loyola Marymount University
Manchester College
Michigan State University Libraries
Middle Tennessee State University
Minuteman Library Network
New Mexico State University
New York Public Library Research
New York University Law School Library
Nova Southeastern University
Ohio State University College of Law
Ohio University
Old Dominion University
Princeton University
Radford University Library
SUNY at Buffalo
Saint Bonaventure University

Seminole Community College
St. Francis University, Pasquerilla Library
Texas A &M University
Texas Southern University Marshall School of Law
Texas State University
Texas Wesleyan University School of Law Library
Tulane University
U.C. Hastings College of Law
US Air Force Academy
US Naval Academy
University of Arizona
University of California,Davis Mabie Law Library
University of Central Florida
University of Delaware
University of Georgia
University of Hawaii at Manoa
University of Iowa Law Library
University of Maryland, College Park
University of Michigan Library
University of Missouri, Columbia
University of North Texas
University of Nebraska, Lincoln
University of Nevada, Reno
University of New Orleans,
University of North Carolina, Chapel Hill
University of Texas, Arlington
University of Utah
University of West Georgia
University of Wisconsin, Oshkosh
University of Wisconsin, Whitewater
Utah State University
Virginia Tech
Washington and Lee University Law Library
Washington College of Law
Western Michigan University
Yale University

Bagnall, Joseph A. *The United states History Abstract: Major Crises in American History.* Kendall Hunt Publishing, 2009

Appendix XI: Hobbies

Writer and Producer

Jazz and Swing Host

Writer and Producer

Since 1983 I have been an independent producer who has placed numerous radio programs on a satellite that beams them to over 300 National Public Radio stations. I have placed many of my own programs on the satellite. My top two programs, in terms of the number of stations that aired them were:

I. Who is Rush Limbaugh? (1993) I wrote, produced and narrated a stinging critique of Rush Limbaugh. It was aired on many NPR stations. I received close to one hundred supportive letters and only one that was critical of my effort.

II. Clean Air Now! Hydrogen as a Fuel (1997). I wrote, produced, and narrated this program. It involved students in SAVE, an environmental club that I advised at MiraCosta College. The students and I engaged in telephone conversations with an expert on hydrogen at the University of Miami and an MD from Riverside, California.

Go to the link for each of these programs on the second page of my website, jabagnall.net, and you can hear them in their entirety.

Jazz and Swing Host

In 2007 I hosted a series of eleven Jazz and swing shows on KKSM, the Palomar College radio station. I have the eleven shows preserved on CDs for my personal use.

Appendix XII:
Heroes and Inspirational Figures

Frank K. Kelly

Frank is listed first because he was a professional associate and he impacted my life personally and directly. I am inspired and uplifted by Frank K, Kelly, former Vice President of the Center for the Study of Democratic Institutions. He was the guiding spirit behind the calling of worldwide "*Pacem in Terris*" conferences based on Pope John XXIII's Encyclical, *Pacem in Terris*. He has been involved throughout his lifetime in the peace movement. In an article in *Saturday Review*, he proposed that the President of the United States should give an annual State of the World address. He is widely recognized for his vision and optimism. The Santa Barbara Nuclear Age Peace Foundation has established the "Frank K. Kelly Annual Lecture on Humanity's Future."

Other Peacemakers

There are many who have contributed to promotion of world peace. We can list some of the contributors and some of their contributions: Woodrow Wilson was the guiding spirit behind the creation of The League of Nations and the United Nations; Wendell Willkie advocated *One World;* Franklin D. Roosevelt worked tirelessly for the founding of the United Nations; Harry Truman and Dwight Eisenhower spoke of a world community under law; Albert Einstein called for world government in an important book, *Einstein on Peace;* Pope John XXIII issued a great Encyclical, *Pacem in Terris;* Mahatma Gandhi and Martin Luther King promoted and practiced non-violent confrontation; Joan B Kroc founded an effective peace institute at the University of San Diego; David Kreiger founded The Nuclear Age Peace foundation in Santa Barbara, and Walter Cronkite has written and spoken of the need for a world peace keeping authority.

All of the above are heroic in their separate pathways to peace. We are all in their debt. Other prominent Peace Makers have contributed in various ways.

Jimmy Carter

As president, Jimmy Carter led a worldwide campaign to promote human rights. He confronted the Soviet Union for violations of the Universal Declaration of Human Rights and boycotted the Moscow Olympics of the 1980s.

In retirement, President Carter has been called upon on numerous occasions to observe and report on procedures utilized in elections around the world. His Carter Center is perhaps the most vital institution in the world in the promotion of peace, justice, and freedom.

As a recipient of the Nobel Peace Prize, he has been duly recognized for his noble work.

Norman Cousins

As editor of *Saturday Review*, Norman Cousins wrote editorials and essays about thermonuclear and environmental issues for over forty years. An advocate of world federalism, he made over 2000 speeches, wrote thousands of editorials and essays, and authored many books calling for world peace through the development of world law. *Modern Man is Obsolete, Who speaks for Man?*, and *In Place of Folly* were three very compelling books on peace.

Cousins was a founder of The National Committee for a Sane Nuclear Policy (SANE); and in the 1960s he became famous for facilitating communication between the Kremlin, the Vatican, and the White House which resulted in the American-Soviet nuclear test ban in the atmosphere. His work on this nuclear test ban is chronicled in his book, *The Improbable Triumvirate.*

For his work on the test ban treaty, Pope John XXIII awarded Cousins his personal medallion. He was also the recipient of the Eleanor Roosevelt Peace Award in 1963, The Family of Man Award in 1968, and The United Nations Peace Medal in 1971. That he was never awarded the Nobel Peace Prize is an incredible oversight.

Norman Cousins shaped my own life more than any other living person When I founded the Fullerton College Center for the Study of the Future of Man, he gave the dedicatory address.

When I was hired as an administrator at Santa Barbara City College, I heard President Bartolazzo report to the Board of Trustees that I had been highly recommended by Mr. Norman Cousins. That was a proud moment that I will always treasure.

John F. Kennedy

President John F. Kennedy is widely regarded as a hawk, a cold warrior, and the president who took us to the brink of nuclear war in the Cuban missile crisis. Missing in most historical and biographical accounts is JFK's unswerving dedication to the building of world peace through world law.

Actually JFK graphically described the power of nuclear weapons and continually warned the American people that nuclear weapons must be controlled. From his salad days as a U.S. Senator to the hour of his death he made heroic proposals for "a grand and global alliance...., a strengthened United Nations...., a world security system...., a worldwide program of conservation...., and world peace through world law."

This Kennedy legacy is found in Alan Nevin's book, *The Strategy of Peace*, a compilation of Senator John F. Kennedy's speeches, and my own books, *President John Fitzgerald Kennedy's Grand and Global Alliance: World Order for the New Century* and *The Kennedy Option Pursuit of World Law.*

The media has cashed in on JFK as a central figure in a murder mystery, as a princely figure in Camelot, and on what should have remained his private life. Meanwhile JFK is much diminished and essentially undiscovered.

John F. Kennedy spoke with urgency and passion about thermonuclear and environmental issues. His words on these subjects are critical in defining the Kennedy legacy. But more importantly, if mankind is to resolve countless life threatening issues, we can no longer ignore *The Kennedy Option: Pursuit of World Law.*

Eleanor Roosevelt

Eleanor Roosevelt served as United States Ambassador to the United Nations in the Truman administration. She was widely admired as the former First Lady, but in her new position most people referred to her as First Lady of the World.

At the United Nations, she became the chairperson of the commission that drafted THE UNIVERSAL DECLARATION OF HUMAN RIGHTS. If James Madison can be called "the Father of the American Bill of Rights," Eleanor Roosevelt must be recognized as the chief architect who reframed those rights and presented them to the entire world.

Every president since December 10, 1945, and President Carter in particular, has reminded other nations of their failures in implementing human rights. The hope for the survival of mankind in a world of peace, justice, and freedom depends upon the swift codification of the ideals of the Universal Declaration of Human Rights into enforceable world law.

A treasured letter from Eleanor Roosevelt follows:

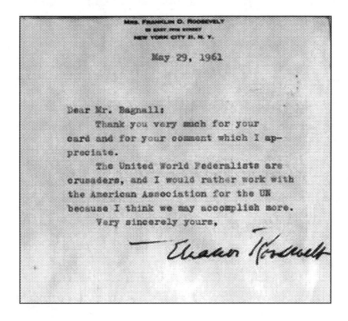

Ted Turner

No living person has matched Ted Turner's efforts in the promotion of peace. He sponsored and financed the Goodwill Games that helped to thaw the chill of the cold war. He has purchased $500 million worth of land with the primary purpose of conserving and preserving species. Turner's commitment to all living things honors Albert Schweitzer's oft quoted phrase, "reverence for life." Turner believes that even bats and rattlesnakes are sacred. He has given $1 billion dollars to the UN and set up a UN foundation; he has established and financed a Nuclear Threat Initiative which has done impressive work in reducing the threat of nuclear, biological and radiological weapons. And in addition to all of this his Turner foundation promotes environmental causes. He is the most generous and compassionate of all the entrepreneurs. Why has he not received the Nobel Peace Prize? He is without question the most deserving of anyone who could currently be considered.

Ted Turner accepted my own television documentary "John F. Kennedy's Lost Pathway to Peace" for airing on TBS, the SuperStation on the 69th and 70th anniversaries of JFK's birth. This TV production documented JFK's persistent call for a strengthened United Nations, the pursuit of world peace through world law and the development of a worldwide program of conservation.

Inspirational Presidents

George Washington

The successes of the American Revolution, the constitutional convention, and the new American Republic, were in large measure due to the superb leadership of George Washington.

Abraham Lincoln

He saved the Union and started African-Americans on their road to freedom and full citizenship.

Theodore Roosevelt

This progressive Republican brought the federal government into new roles in conservation of natural resources, regulating railroads, building dams, and protecting the consumer against contaminated foods and medicines.

His leadership resulted in the emergence of the United States as a world power with a two-ocean navy and an isthmian canal connecting the two great oceans.

Woodrow Wilson

This progressive Democrat presided over the creation of the Federal Trade Commission and the Federal Reserve System.

Joseph A. Bagnall

He also gave the world a formula for peace and paved the way for the creation of the United Nations

Franklin D. Roosevelt

FDR worked with Winston Churchill to establish the United Nations. In addition he guided the ratification of this great institution to a smashing 89 to 2 victory in the United States Senate. His New Deal did not solve the Great Depression, but it prevented the complete collapse of the United States economy, thereby saving American capitalism. He led the allies to victory in World War II, thereby playing the key role in the saving of Western civilization

John F. Kennedy

He set the goal for a moon landing and marshaled the forces that brought it about.
He was also dedicated to the idea of world peace through the development of world law.

Appendix XIII:
Ashley Jo Bagnall

Ashley Jo Bagnall
   Age 4
4249 Mesa Vista Way
Oceanside, CA 92056

SCARECROW

Ashley Jo Bagnall Age 8

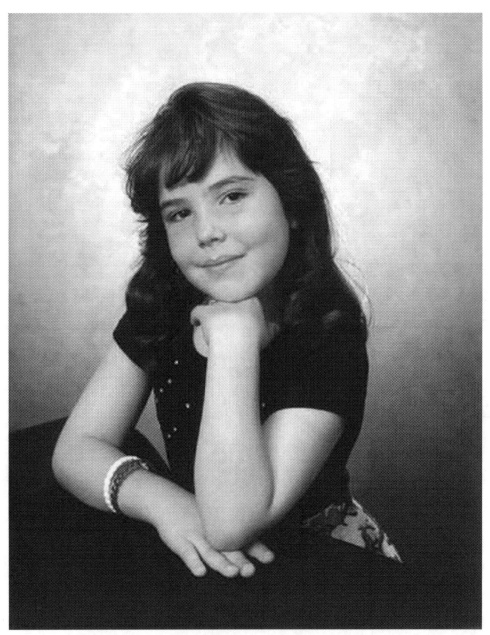

Ashley Jo Bagnall Age 8

Ashley in her Brownie uniform.

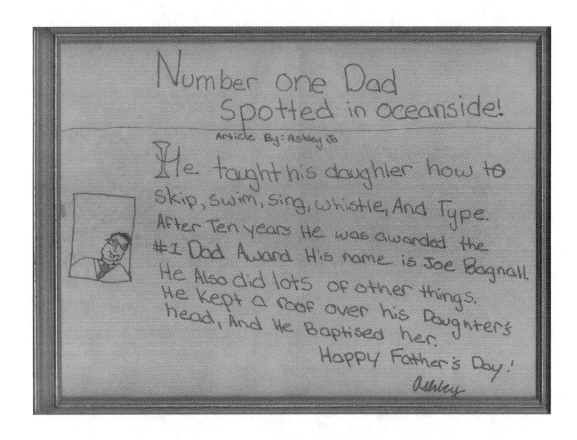

MATHEMATICS AND VERBAL TALENT SEARCH

conducted by the
Institute for the Academic Advancement of Youth (IAAY)

STATE AWARD

THE JOHNS HOPKINS UNIVERSITY

Presented to

ASHLEY BAGNALL

for being among the highest scoring participants in the

STATE OF CALIFORNIA
1997

Mathematics and Verbal Talent Search.

William R. Brody
President
The Johns Hopkins University

Steven Knapp
Provost
The Johns Hopkins University

William G. Durden
Executive Director of IAAY
The Johns Hopkins University

Ashley Jo Bagnall

El Camino High School - Extra Curricular Highlights

Speech and Debate
- o Began competing for the school debate team in grade 10
- o President of the debate team in grades 10 and 11
- o Debate captain in grade 12
- o Placed in the state championships in grades 11 and 12
- o Speech Department Award, 1999-2000
- o Best Debater Award, 1999-2000
- o Team Player Award, 1999-2000
- o Outstanding Varsity Award, 2000-2001
- o All time school leader in the number of speech and debate trophies won

Drama
- o Involved in several school plays from grades 9 through 11
- o Had the female lead roles in two plays: Rachel, in Inherit the Wind and Beatrice, in Much Ado About Nothing.

Dance
- o Member of the school Dance Club in grades 11 and 12
- o Participated in two end of year dance performances

Academics
- o Member of the National Honor Roll
- o Member of and Master of Ceremonies for the school University Club Attended the National Student Leadership Conference held at American University, in the summer of 2001

Statement on Father's Day 2005

A few years ago, Apple Computers borrowed the rights to use the images of a few famous crusaders for Justice: Bobby Kennedy, Martin Luther King, Jr., Eleanor Roosevelt, Cesar Chavez, and Franklin D. Roosevelt. Their advertisements would feature one of these famous portraits next to a modest Apple logo and the pithy slogan, "think different." The message almost seemed to capitalize on the brand's unpopularity. It was as if, by using Apple Computers, the average Joe Blow places himself above the mediocrity of the PC mainstream. He becomes capable of challenging the status quo with his sophisticated choice in technology. Like Gandhi, the Apple consumer is capable of achieving great things; of becoming a legend.

In the summer of 2000, Apple created a huge mural on the side of the Hotel Figueroa in Los Angeles, bearing all five of those famous faces. The Democratic National Convention was nominating Al Gore at the Staples Center just a few blocks away, and Rage Against the Machine was about to hold a concert protesting the two-party system somewhere in the streets in between the two. I was fifteen.

Maybe it was an excuse to be near all that political tension in the air, or maybe it's just because the mural was so larger-than-life, but my dad, a history professor by occupation and by birth, wanted to drive up to L.A. for an afternoon to see it. When I told a friend where we were going, there was dead silence on the phone for a beat. "You're driving to Los Angeles... to see an ad for Apple Computers?"

We bought a disposable camera at a dark, cramped drugstore. Walking the streets, it was apparent that there was something big going on. There were reporters buzzing around to interview the drugstore owner, huge cameras weighing down one shoulder or the other, and there were barricades on all the streets, channeling the chaotic flow of traffic around The Event. In preparation for the concert and other protests, there was information for citizens providing instructions on how to stay safe in the event that police should need to use tear gas. We walked down to the Staples center to observe the whirr of activity outside of it. My dad nearly gushed enthusiasm to the campaign workers, asking if there was anything he could do to help.

I don't remember any of the specific questions I asked him that day, but I'm sure my curious mind was intrigued by the things that were going on in that chaotic five-block radius. And I distinctly remember that my dad had answers and explanations to all my curious inquiries. Suddenly, politics seemed a little more interesting, a little more tangible.

We took pictures of the Staples Center, and of the Apple ad. I took pictures of my father standing in front of the hotel, hands on hips, with the broad, confident smile of one who is in his element; one with conviction. It's my favorite picture of my dad. In the photograph, his head almost covers up the Apple logo, so that he appears to be pictured alongside Kennedy, Roosevelt, Chavez, King, Gandhi. In my heart of hearts, I feel that he deserves to be among them.

He has retired from teaching twice, but he has never actually quit. He is seventy-five years old and he sometimes accepts a 150% assignment. At the end of one teaching year he exceeded his earnings limitation and could not be paid for much of his work. He reported that news to my mother and me with the same amount of disappointment he might show if he had broken a dish or missed a green light. It's always been obvious to us that his work is its own reward.

The last time I saw my dad, he ranted and raved about the Bush administration for a few minutes before he started in on a story about a Utah farm boy named Philo T. Farnsworth, the inventor of television. Farnsworth, my dad tells me, came up with the idea of TV when he was 14, and had actually built one before he was my age. The idea for the television was stolen by RCA, and Farnsworth never received compensation or credit for his idea. Farnsworth grew up so bitter that he refused to ever own a television.

My dad explained all of this to my mother and I, who sat, elbows on the table, chins in hands, glazed looks in our eyes. "Is there a reason you always choose depressing things to talk about?" I asked, trying to lighten the mood. You can't be as passionate as my father is about history, politics, and teaching without also being deeply hurt when those things disappoint you, and I've seen my father become enraged or even depressed when he is discouraged politically, or when the occasional student flakes out on his classes.

My dad has the ability to energize and inspire many students. I've lost track of how many times my dad has shared letters or emails with me from former students, thanking him profusely for his help, thanking him for making history relevant and interesting, thanking him for going out of his way to help the students to succeed in the course. I can't tell you how many times I've heard things like "your class was my first college A, and now I'm studying for the Bar exam," or "before your class I had a 2.0 grade point average, but you showed me I was capable of doing a lot better." Former students talk about him like this all the time.

Driving home from L.A. that afternoon, my questions led into a lecture about the Cuban Missile Crisis. Suddenly, all the John F. Kennedy campaign posters that my dad used to collect and display in his den made so much sense. I could understand, really understand, the dilemma that Kennedy was facing. It's not an exaggeration to say that the fate of the world rested in his hands, and there was no way of knowing the possible outcome of his actions. Kennedy was blessed with skill, intelligence, and luck in averting nuclear war. As my dad related his personal memories of the incident, I understood how monumental the situation was. There he was, a high school teacher at the time, and the whole world was tuned to the news to see what would happen when The Confrontation came. The principal of the school decided to be safe by sounding the alarm, so that everyone could get under their desks, just in case. Children were crying. Teachers didn't know what to do. Everyone thought that they were being attacked with nuclear weapons. Suddenly I understood that the Cuban Missile Crisis was called a crisis for a reason, and I remember gazing out the car window as the freeway scenery rolled by, literally seeing the world in a whole new light, shaped by an incipient appreciation for history. It was so amazing to me that the "tyrant" who just didn't understand anything, suddenly did understand, and know, so much.

I never have any idea what to get my dad for Father's Day. The gifts pushed onto me as a consumer every year never seem to fit. My dad doesn't golf, he's far from a fix-it man, and he doesn't drink beer. He's just not a stereotypical father. But really, he's much better.

But even buying him something related to his interests seems inadequate. Somehow, buying a hardcover biography of JFK just seems insufficient to present to a man who has a framed card signed by Kennedy when he served in the Senate, thanking my father for encouraging him to run for President. A portrait of RFK just isn't an adequate gift for a man who cried for three days straight after the man was assassinated.

My mom and I usually end up taking my dad out to dinner on Father's Day, and he usually selects a humble restaurant and is grateful for the gesture and the time spent with us. Every year on Father's Day, I try to explain to my dad just how much he means to me, just how proud of him am, how I want to be like him, because I figure these things are more important than gifts, but my words are so inadequate over the clinking of glasses and clanging of silverware.

In describing this one afternoon that I shared with my father, I hope maybe I can give him a glimpse of the person I see in him. When I think about him as a father, I will always remember the summers he drove me all the way to Utah for BYU summer camps, and I will always remember the long rides home from school when I thought I hated him for lecturing me for my own good. There were the basketball games every January at SDSU, and I'll always remember him taking me out to eat and making me drink milk, even in high school. I'll always remember his strictness about my music, clothes, and friends, and then there were the times that he would take me to get my hair done right before we took a daddy/daughter picture together.

I'll always remember him walking me down the aisle at my wedding, and the overnight stops in Las Vegas where we would catch shows at Circus Circus and have our portraits drawn by airbrush artists on the street.

But for some reason, that one dusty summer afternoon in Los Angeles will always stand out in my mind.

Happy Father's Day, Teed.